John Diodati's Doctrine of Holy Scripture

Reformed Historical-Theological Studies

General Editors
Joel R. Beeke and Jay T. Collier

The Christology of John Owen
by Richard W. Daniels

The Covenant Theology of Caspar Olevianus
by Lyle D. Bierma

John Diodati's Doctrine of Holy Scripture
by Andrea Ferrari

John Diodati's Doctrine of Holy Scripture

considered especially on the basis of his
Theses theologicae de Sacra Scriptura of 1596

Andrea Ferrari

REFORMATION HERITAGE BOOKS, INC.
Grand Rapids, Michigan USA

© 2006 by Andrea Ferrari

Published by
Reformation Heritage Books
2965 Leonard St. NE
Grand Rapids, MI 49525
616-977-0599 / Fax 616-285-3246
e-mail: orders@heritagebooks.org
website: www. heritagebooks.org

10 digit ISBN #1-892777-98-3
13 digit ISBN #978-1-892777-98-0

For additional Reformed literature, both new and used, request a free booklist from Reformation Heritage Books as the above address

AUTHOR'S PREFACE

This study considers important aspects of the work of John Diodati (1576-1649), one of the epigones of Calvin and Beza, who served as pastor of the Italian church in Geneva and professor at Calvin's Academy. Particular attention is given to his doctrine of Scripture, not only because of the controversy concerning the authority of the Bible that was an essential part of the Reformation, but also because Diodati was responsible for an influential translation of the Bible into Italian.

This study begins with a discussion of the state of research on Diodati. This is followed by a survey of Diodati's life and work, focusing on his role within contemporary Protestantism. The history of the doctrine of Scripture is then considered in order to provide the relevant background to Diodati's beliefs and to the significance of Scripture in the disputes that were part and parcel of the Reformation. The central element of the dissertation consists of a translation from Latin into English of the twenty-five theses concerning the doctrine of Scripture that he presented in 1596, when he graduated from the Academy at Geneva. There follows a detailed analysis of these theses in the light of the Protestant view of Scripture and the controversy with the teaching of the Church of Rome, especially as set out in the formulations of the Council of Trent. This analysis also draws on a work for which Diodati was well known to the English public, namely his *Pious Annotations upon the Holy Bible*, his greatest legacy after his translation of the Italian Bible. The study concludes with a brief evaluation of the significance of the continuity of the doctrine of Scripture in the history of the church, of the debate over the issue of authority between the Reformers and Rome, and of the way in which Diodati's attitude to the translation of Scripture was governed by both the need for clarity and the theology of the Bible itself.

TABLE OF CONTENTS

Introduction 1
   The state of research on John Diodati

Chapter 1 5
   A biographical sketch of John Diodati

Chapter 2 22
   The doctrine of Scripture: a historical survey

Chapter 3 46
   A translation of Diodati's *Theses theologicae de Sacra Scriptura*

Chapter 4 52
   Diodati's doctrine of Scripture in his *Theses theologicae de Sacra Scriptura:* a theological and historical commentary, with additional reference to Diodati's *Pious Annotations on the Holy Bible*

Conclusion 103

Notes 109

Bibliography 123

INTRODUCTION

One of the many Italian refugees in Geneva "for the sake of religion" (*religionis causa*) at the time of the Reformation, John Diodati is best known as the man who provided the only Italian Bible available to the people of Italy after 1559, the year when Pope Paul IV prohibited the possession and printing of any sort of vernacular Bible. Diodati's Bible, first published in 1607, eventually became the standard version of the Scriptures for Italian Protestants. But he is also important for other reasons: indeed, his work as professor at the Academy in Geneva, his pastoral ministry in the citadel of Protestantism, his participation at the Synod of Dort, and his involvement in the social and political life of seventeenth-century Europe make him an outstanding personality of that era.

Despite Diodati's significance as a major theologian, Bible translator, and figurehead of the Reformation's Italian refugees, however, comparatively little attention has been given to him by scholars. The general consensus of scholars concerning the state of research on Diodati may be summed up in the words of William McComish: "There has not been any considerable amount of work devoted to Diodati, and not all that has been published can be regarded as satisfactory."[1] The relevance of this statement appears especially evident if the many substantial volumes published with regard to the sixteenth century and its chief protagonists are compared with the few about Diodati and other important figures of the seventeenth century. Nevertheless, in recent years there has been an increasing interest in Diodati's life and work, as well as in the period during which he lived. Of particular importance—because it is the only academic work available in English on Diodati—is the volume of the above-mentioned William McComish, *The Epigones: a study of the theology of the Genevan Academy at the time of the Synod of Dort, with special reference to Giovanni Diodati*, published in 1989. The author, however, states that his study "remains introductory in character."[2] To this author's knowledge, the only other English work devoted to John Diodati is the short *Life of Giovanni Diodati, Genevese Theologian, translator of the Italian Bible*.[3]

Although there are more volumes on Diodati in French and Italian, scholars of these two countries have not yet responded to McComish's assertion that "there is room for a major work concerning Diodati, or at least, a series of specialised articles."[4] In those studies published, expressions of uncertainty and comments on the paucity of documentation are quite common. Thus far, *Vie de Jean Diodati, Theologien Genevois*, written by Eugène de Budé and published in Lousanne in 1869, has been regarded as the standard French biography of Diodati.[5] Another interesting work in French is *Jean Diodati à Nimes 1614*,[6] which describes Diodati's work in the church of Nimes in order to bring stability after the excommunication of the pastor, Jérémie Furrier. Mention should also be made of *Calvin and Diodati, essay de comparison portant sur la predestination*.[7]

Other significant works, though not directly concerned with the life of Diodati, are: *Histoire de l'Eglise de Genève*;[8] *Les Pasteurs génevois d'origine lucquoise*;[9] *Le refugée Italien de Genève aux XVIe et XVIIe siècles*;[10] *Nicolas Antoine, un pasteur protestant brulé à Genève en 1632 pour crime de judaisme*;[11] *Histoire de l'Université de Genève*;[12]

L'Eglise de Genève;[13] and *Un itinéraire spirituelle au XVIIe siècle, Nicolas Antoine 1602?-1632.*[14]

In Italy, Milka Ventura has been the most prolific writer on the life and work of John Diodati. Her research differs in character from that of McComish, being more philological than theological. Her first work is an unpublished graduate thesis, entitled "L'esegesi del Genesi e la teologia della Riforma: due commentari a confronto: Brucioli e Diodati."[15] This work is divided into three volumes and two parts. The first volume contains biographies of John Diodati and of Antonio Brucioli,[16] together with her evaluation of their two commentaries. The other volumes analyze and compare the comments by Brucioli and Diodati on various passages of Genesis. Her second major work is the unpublished doctoral dissertation, "Giovanni Diodati e le traduzioni della Bibbia nel suo tempo: l'Antico Testamento."[17] In this study, Ventura sets Diodati in his historical background. She begins by examining what she considers to be a decline in the study of the original languages for the sake of theological debate. In her judgment, the so-called Protestant Orthodoxy is the champion of a method that reads too much into texts in order to support doctrinal interpretations. She shows that Diodati is caught in a controversial debate over three major topics: the controversy concerning translations, the problem of the text, and the question of the Hebrew tradition. She also makes some linguistic and theological comparisons between Diodati's versions of the Bible[18] and other versions, such as the Vulgate and the King James.

More recently, Ventura, together with Michele Ranchetti, edited *La Bibbia di Diodati.*[19] This new edition of Diodati's translation of the Bible is the result of meticulous research over more than fifteen years. Four introductory essays preface Diodati's Bible itself. The first, by Ranchetti, is a short general introduction to Diodati's life and work; the second, by Ventura, focuses on Diodati as a translator; the third, by Sergio Bozzola, is concerned with the language and style of Diodati's Bible; and the final contribution, by Emidio Campi, is a well documented and lengthy chronology of Diodati's life.

There are other significant writings by Italian scholars, all of which are referred to in the bibliographies of the above-mentioned works.[20] The most important of these are as follows: *Giovanni Diodati il Traduttore della Bibbia e la Società degli Esuli Protestanti Italiani a Ginevra;*[21] *La Bibbia in Italia. L'Eco della Riforma nella Repubblica Lucchese: Giovanni Diodati e la sua Traduzione Italiana della Bibbia;*[22] and *Giovanni Diodati e la sua Attività Ecclesiastica.*[23]

The purpose of this thesis (University of Wales, Lampeter, 2003) is to analyze Diodati's doctrine of Holy Scripture, considered especially on the basis of his *Theses theologicae de Sacra Scriptura* of 1596. There is good reason to conclude that these twenty-five theological theses on the doctrine of the Word of God are crucial for understanding Diodati's life and work. Therefore, following McComish's suggestion concerning the need for a number of specialized studies, this book considers in some depth this fundamental aspect of Diodati's thought, which was already rooted in his mind when he was twenty years of age.

CHAPTER

1

A Biographical Sketch of John Diodati

In the third quarter of the sixteenth century, many Italian families were obliged to flee from the Tuscan republic of Lucca because of great persecution by the Roman Inquisition aimed at crushing the impressive success of the evangelical doctrines of the Reformation.[24] It seems that "almost all the leading families [of Lucca] had a Reformed person in the house."[25] This movement of refugees, begun in 1542, increased especially in 1555 and lasted for more than two decades.[26]

The Diodatis were one of the wealthiest families of Lucca.[27] Michele Diodati was a doctor and a businessman, as well as a very educated man. He had served a number of terms as Gonfalonier of Justice and as Elder of the city. He was very open to the preaching of the Reformers; in fact, in 1558, he was called to Rome and the Inquisition compelled him to confess his loyalty to the Pope. His son, Carlo, was born in Lucca in September 1541, at the same time that Pope Paul III and the Emperor Charles V were meeting in the city of Lucca to discuss Lutherans, Turks, and the coming general council of the Roman Catholics. One night, the Emperor was awakened by the sound of people coming and going and by the cries of someone in pain. He was told that a noble woman, Anna Bonvisi, wife of Michele Diodati, was giving birth to a baby. Charles V wanted to stand as godfather to the child, giving him his own name. The Pope conducted the ritual and the little boy was named Carlo (Charles).[28] Surely neither "representative of God" who came to Lucca to crush the "Lutheran hydra" could have imagined that their godson would be the father of John Diodati, the most influential promoter of the Reformation in Italy.[29] Carlo Diodati fled to Geneva in 1567 and, in March 1568, was declared a heretic by Rome.

John Diodati was born in Geneva at the beginning of June 1576.[30] Little information is available on his childhood and adolescence. Nevertheless, it is quite clear that in his home and among other Italian refugees he had an example of faith in and zeal for the evangelical doctrines of the Reformation, industriousness, simplicity, modesty, and a sense of duty. After the normal studies at the Genevan College to acquire familiarity with the classics, he attended the Genevan Academy to study biblical and theological disciplines.

The nature of Geneva's Academy casts much light on Diodati's life and work. Its basic aim was declared in 1637 by the pastors and professors of Geneva, among whom was Diodati: "It is not good that our students should be vain disputants, or that they should be learned in a theory without savour or strength. *The true aim which we should set before ourselves…is to provide a holy nursery-garden of devout pastors,* pure in their faith, strong in their zeal to teach, well conducted and sober, keeping guard with a clear conscience over the grand mystery of piety, and administering with justice the Word of Truth."[31] This statement accurately reflects the original vision of John Calvin (1509-1564). According to the Ecclesiastical Ordinances of 1541, the College he wished to see established was to serve the purpose of preparing children "for both the ministry and civil government."[32]

At both the College and the Academy, young people were educated in the so-called humanities. Although "the education offered in the College and Academy was in many ways typically humanistic,"[33] from the very beginnings, in Geneva as in Calvin's own life, "humanistic studies were to be directed to the service of the Word of God."[34] Calvin did not disdain secular human learning, as is evident from reading his *Institutes* and commentaries. Nevertheless, he made it ancillary to biblical interpretation and theological reflection. In other words, at the Academy of Geneva, philosophy, philology, and the other sciences were studied within the context of biblical faith, rather than for their own sake. Louis Binz explains as follows: "Religious teaching had an important place. Each lesson opened and closed with prayer. One hour during the day was kept for sacred hymns. On Wednesday mornings pupils listened to a sermon that they had to discuss in the afternoons. On Sundays...they attended a morning service, an afternoon service and the catechising."[35] While Calvin's humanism was apparent in the program of the Academy, "it must be kept in mind that he was definitely not a humanist in his interpretation of the origins and source of man's capacity...." Moreover, "Calvin's view was that these arts and sciences discovered by man were not to be used for the glorification and praise of human genius, but for the glory of God."[36] The leaders of reform in Geneva were not anti-humanists yet; in spite of their participation in the Renaissance movement, they were believers in the doctrines of original sin and of the supremacy of Scripture over human reason. Calvin's spiritual journey caused him to pass through Rome and Athens, but his destination was Jerusalem.

The influence of the Academy may be illustrated from the time of great revival and church growth in France.[37] At the end of 1555, there were only five organized churches in France, but by the beginning of 1562, there were 1,785. In this period, eighty-eight pastors had been recommended and sent out by the Venerable Company to the French churches. Many of these men were trained at the Academy of Geneva, which was opened in 1559. These pastors "managed to organise religious discontent in France into a militant church in less than a decade.... The training that these men received in Geneva must have been exceptionally effective, teaching them not only how to do their pastoral work well, but also how to co-operate with one another with uncommon efficiency."[38] Robert M. Kingdon says: "A program of intense study was required of all candidates for the Calvinist ministry in France. One of the sources of the Reformation had been the scholarly, critical study of the Bible, and each Calvinist minister was expected to be well equipped for the continuing task of biblical study and exegesis.... Only a man with a high degree of linguistic and philological ability could be entrusted with the task of interpreting to less learned and otherwise occupied people the very words of Almighty God."[39] These students, however, were not accredited as missionaries after mere academic training. The Company of Pastors not only examined the candidates doctrinally but also made serious enquiries as to their way of life.[40] This, therefore, was the environment in which Diodati's life was shaped.

In 1596, at the end of his formal education at the Academy, Diodati submitted his twenty-five theological theses on the Holy Scriptures. In these theses, "we recognize the agenda of an entire existence."[41] Emidio Campi argues that "this theme will reveal itself of central importance in his [Diodati's] future work."[42] The

Biographical Sketch 9

following year, Diodati was called to teach Hebrew at the Academy, and at the end of 1599, he was also occupying the chair of theology, though not full time. Borgeaud, in his monumental and highly influential *Histoire de l'Université de Genève*, stresses that these appointments were the result especially of the social influence of his family and of the aim of Antoine de la Faye to be the recognized successor of Beza (1519-1605). Borgeaud intended to assert that the independence of the chair of Hebrew and Greek at this time was lost in order to subordinate them to that of theology.[43] Emidio Campi, however, is not so sure about the weight to be ascribed to the social position of the Diodatis and to the academic and ecclesiastical intrigues of the period,[44] and believes that two important factors must be kept in mind. First of all, Geneva experienced economic difficulties during the years 1589-1602 as a consequence of the war against Savoy. Geneva was under siege for a long time, and this situation motivated the authorities to save as much money as they could. For this reason, the income of pastors and professors alike was reduced, making it impossible for the Academy to replace the old professors with acclaimed and prestigious new instructors; the only possible course of action was to discover new local talents and use them. Secondly, the more mature professors were increasingly engaged in polemics and apologetics, and as a result they neglected the field of biblical philology.

At the end of 1600, Diodati married Maddalena Burlamacchi—another child of refugees from Lucca—who would present her husband with nine children. In 1603, he submitted a proof of his Italian translation of the Bible to the Company of Pastors. It seems that he began this work when he was only sixteen years of age. After further work on the accuracy and style of his version, it was published in 1607 under the title of *La Bibbia, cioè i libri del Vecchio e del Nuovo Testamento nuovamente traslati in lingua Italiana da Giovanni Diodati di nation Lucchese.*[45] In July 1607, Diodati wrote to the French historian Jacques Auguste de Thou: "The favourable judgment that you have been pleased to make on the sample of my rendering of the Italian Bible...has been of great guidance and comfort in the pursuit of this great labour that I began in my first youth.... I took utmost care, with all my powers and with the most careful conscience of which I have been able, in order to open to our Italians the door of the knowledge of celestial truth.... Our Lord, who has miraculously led and strengthened me in this work, will make it strong with his blessing."[46] During these years, Diodati corresponded with the English ambassador in Venice, Sir Henry Watton, whom he had met in Geneva. From their letters it seems that the young professor had in his heart a great desire to see Italy conquered by the evangelical doctrines of the Reformation, and that he considered Venice an open door. His work on the translation of the Bible into Italian developed and grew parallel with the consciousness of Italians' need for free and direct access to the Holy Scriptures without any kind of restriction. Although there is no clear evidence concerning what actually moved Diodati in this endeavor, there are a number of factors that partially explain his motivation and zeal.

First, Diodati's own conception of the nature of Scripture was of particular significance. In his 1596 theological thesis, *De Sacra Scriptura*, he affirms that Holy Scripture is the divinely inspired Word of God that imparts "all necessary knowledge for eternal life."[47] Therefore, uppermost in his young mind was the consciousness that the Bible was a word from God Himself, and that its message was necessary for the salvation of sinners.

Secondly, from his childhood he was closely involved in the Genevan efforts to counteract schemes of Rome aimed at nullifying the results of the Reformation in Europe. It is important to remember the story of the Diodatis and of many other Italian refugees in Geneva "for the sake of religion" (*religionis causa*). How could his heart not be deeply involved in the defense of the truths of the gospel for which his grandfather, his father, and many other people from Lucca and other parts of Italy suffered so much, and for which they had to flee their country? His training in the spiritual environment of the Genevan Academy was also important in this respect. In Geneva, the students lived in an atmosphere of excitement and tension, because it was "at the same time the city of refuge and the school of the martyr."[48] Diodati must have known about the secret missionary activities on behalf of Europe coordinated by the pastors and professors in Geneva; the hidden traffic of Bibles and literature from Geneva to Italy, especially through Venice; and the many missionary-martyrs like Giacomo Bonello and Gian Luigi Pascale, whom the church in Geneva had sent to Italy.

The direction of Diodati's life and work was also determined by the decisions of Rome concerning translations of the Bible. In April 1546, the Council of Trent decided to receive the sacred books of the Old and New Testaments (including the Apocrypha), with the usage of the Vulgate, as the only common official version of the Bible.[49] The Council had been silent on the matter of vernacular translations because it was divided into two factions over the issue.[50] This problem was resolved with the ascent of Gian Piero Carafa to the Papal throne in 1555, taking the name of Paul IV. It was Carafa who, in 1542, organized the Inquisition. As soon as possible, he gave a mandate to a commission composed of faithful members of the Inquisition to prepare a catalog of prohibited books. Therefore, in 1559, Rome officially declared for the first time a restriction on the printing, reading, and possession of the Bible in vernacular form without the special permission of the Inquisition.[51]

After the death of Paul IV, the so-called *Index Tridentinus* was promulgated under the pontificate of Pius IV. Some changes were included in this index, mainly to give back to the bishops the power they had lost because of the Index of Paul IV, which made the inquisitors the supreme authority. The most significant alteration was that permission to print, read, and possess the Bible in the vernacular was the prerogative not only of the inquisitors but also of the bishops; either could authorize people to read an approved Catholic version of the Bible to increase their faith and piety after having consulted the local priests. But this minor amendment was short-lived. After a period of internal struggle between the bishops and the Congregation of Inquisition, vernacular versions of the Bible were definitively forbidden with the promulgation of the *Index Clementinus* in 1596, the very same year in which Diodati completed his theses on the Holy Scriptures.

These developments undoubtedly shaped the vision of the young John Diodati, and in particular, his concern for Italy and his efforts to develop relationships in Venice. The above-mentioned Sir Henry Watton, English ambassador in Venice, was keen to introduce the evangelical doctrines of the Reformation there, and asked for Diodati's help. Venice was the place that offered the greatest freedom from the influence and control of Rome. Diodati wrote to Philippe Duplessis-Mornay, the Huguenot leader, saying, "I resolved to follow this holy and desirable work."[52] In August 1608, he left for Venice,[53] but was quite disappointed in his hopes. In fact Frà (friar) Paolo Sarpi,[54] "the chief instrumental wheel in this holy affair," failed "to open a breach." In a detailed written report to Sir Henry Watton, Diodati lamented that many people became "cold," seeing Frà Paolo "conniving and deeply dissimulating the faith he professed."[55]

The following is Diodati's own judgement on Frà Paolo: "He is a perfect politician, jurisconsult, theologian and also a doctor, but this great learning is mixed with such a scrupulous prudence and so little warmed and sharpened by zeal of spirit—though his life is right and exemplary—that I do not consider him able to fire the mine in order to open a breach."[56] Diodati did not find a sufficient number of people willing to unite and profess "piety." His conclusion, therefore, was that "God will have to give birth to this circumstance at another time or by someone else who, in the strength of his own authority, may be brought to act."

Upon his return home in November 1608, Diodati was ordained to the pastoral ministry. In a letter to his friend, Duplessis-Mornay, he says concerning his call to the ministry: "I accepted not without much fear and anxiety, which caused me to be very perplexed, until I resolved to put aside my reason and judgements in order to be led by the constraint and the strength of the calling of God...[and] shall labor to imitate every day the holy example of the great servants of God."[57] According to the Registers of the Consistory, Diodati had "always desired" to enter the Christian ministry according to "the vow of his parents since his youth."[58]

Diodati's attitude to his pastoral work was linked to his great ability as an exegete. His skill in this respect was reflected both in preaching and in giving spiritual direction, as illustrated by the blend of exegetical theology and spiritual application that characterizes his *Pious and Learned Annotations* on the Bible, which "reveal a pietistic and non-dogmatic emphasis."[59] Diodati was also pastorally wise and tactful. In 1612, the church of

Nimes asked the Company of Pastors in Geneva to send him to help them after the abjuration of the pastor Jérémie Ferrier. After much persistence on the part of the church, this request was accepted on the condition that his stay in Nimes should not last longer than six months. After the excommunication of Ferrier, Diodati left Geneva at the end of April 1614, and in a few months he was able to restore order and discipline to the church.[60] The same circumstance was repeated in 1617, when Diodati spent six months in Pont-de-Veyle. He exercised a ministry "of reconciliation that left visible signs and deep gratitude."[61]

As for his preaching, it seems that Diodati was renowned all over Europe for his eloquence. Renato Coisson reports that he was known as the "Cato of Geneva."[62] While attending the Synod of Dordrecht (1618-1619), Diodati had many opportunities to preach. The Scottish delegate Baulcanquhall commented that Diodati "did very sweetly just as he useth to preach, not as Doctors use to do in Schools."[63] His preaching was passionate, courageous, and applicatory, as illustrated by an event late in Diodati's life. In the Genevan election of 1645, there were grievous abuses and electoral frauds. Campi explains that this was not an "unexpected" incident, for it had been impossible to restrain social and moral decline. Diodati himself had many times preached in defense of the public good. Now, at 69 years of age, the old pastor preached a "powerful exhortation" to the Council of the Two Hundred. Though rebuked because of his attempts to interfere in political issues, in January 1649, he preached yet another disturbing sermon, denouncing a situation where "fools govern the wise."[64]

The government of Geneva, together with the Company of Pastors, chose Diodati for a diplomatic mission to France. Geneva needed financial help to repair its walls because the city was seriously threatened by the Duke of Savoy. After this successful journey, Diodati began—with Benedetto Turettini[65]—to preach regularly for six years for the Italian church in Geneva that had remained without a pastor. His willingness to undertake this additional task is further evidence of his pastoral devotion and ability.

As mentioned above, Diodati attended the famous Synod of Dordrecht, which had been summoned because of a grave theological dispute caused by the views of Jacobus Arminius (1560-1609). Arminius was initially a staunch Calvinist who studied under Beza at Geneva and Gomarus at Leyden, but his views began to change and he reached the point of affirming that the election of a believer is not grounded on divine sovereign grace but on his foreseen faith. Arminius was particularly opposed to Beza's schematization concerning God's election,[66] and ended up opposing Reformed theology by teaching that man is able to cooperate with God in his salvation.

Arminius died in 1609 at the height of the controversy. Those who agreed with him—the so-called Arminians—went further than Arminius and, in 1610, they drew up a five-point document known as the Remonstrance. In this document, they asked for a correction of the doctrinal standards of the church, namely, the Belgic Confession and the Heidelberg Catechism. After a conference between the two parties in 1611, the Contra-Remonstrants sought to bring about a national synod that, after many civil intrigues, was finally convened in November 1618, at Dordrecht. As a Genevan representative, Diodati was held in much esteem and, together with the other Genevan, Theodore Tronchin, he made an important contribution to the work of the Synod. McComish lists eight different categories of "minor contributions" made by Diodati and

Tronchin,[67] in addition to their deep involvement in the formulation of the five canons, or answers, of the Synod to the five remonstrances of the Arminians. Diodati was also a member of the committee that was called to formulate the Canons after having given due consideration to the doctrines of the Remonstrants and to the answers conveyed by each delegation present at the Synod.[68]

After these events, the Company of Pastors and the Professors of the Academy—among whom was Diodati—were engaged in a controversy with the Jesuits over the Genevan translations of the Bible. The subtle and tenacious opposition of the Jesuits to these translations was provoked by the prosperity of the Reformed cause in France. The attacks by Francois Veron and especially by Pierre Coton[69] were aimed at destroying the confidence of the people in the fidelity of the Protestants to Scripture.[70] One of the chief accusations of the Catholics was that the many versions and interpretations of the Bible showed the inability of the Protestants to find common agreement on the meaning of that Word to whose authority they claimed to submit. This dispute gave rise to those prejudices against the French translation of the Bible by Diodati that will be discussed later.

In 1625, Carlo Diodati—the father of John—died, and his wife, Maria Mei, died the following year. They were to their son an example of faith, diligence, modesty, and sense of duty. In subsequent years, beside his regular duties, Diodati was engaged in diplomatic negotiations with Zurich in order to ask for food on behalf of Geneva, and with Valtellina in Northern Italy, in order to help the Reformed people in that region. In 1631, he completed his rendering of the Psalms in Italian to be sung in the Italian churches of Europe.[71] In 1632, Diodati was involved in the "Antoine case." Nicolas Antoine had studied theology at the Academy and became pastor in Divonne. In addition to conducting himself in a manner not suitable to his ministerial position, Antoine came very close to Judaism by repudiating the Christian doctrines regarding the person of Jesus Christ. Diodati was among those most determined to deal firmly with him; in February 1632, Antoine was burned at the stake. This event had a significant impact on Diodati, much as the Servetus case had on Calvin.

In 1634, another theological controversy broke out, this time in France. The dispute was related to the doctrine of election, with special reference to the concept of particular redemption as taught in the Canons of Dordrecht, which affirmed that "Jesus Christ hath not suffered death, but for the elect only; having neither any intent nor commandment from the Father, to make satisfaction for the sins of the whole world."[72] The contention broke out with the publication of the *Brief Traitté de la prédestination et de ses principales dépendances* by Moise Amyraut (1596-1664), a professor of the Academy of Saumur that had been founded by Diodati's friend, Philippe Duplessis-Mornay. In his treatise, Amyraut expounded the so-called "hypothetical redemption," according to which the Father sent Christ into the world "as a universal remedy to procure salvation for each and every one under the condition of faith." He affirmed that "the redemption of Christ is to be considered in two ways: either as absolute, inasmuch as some truly embrace it; again as it is affected by a condition, inasmuch as it is offered on these terms – that if anyone will embrace it, he shall become partaker of it. In the former mode, it is particular; in the latter, universal."[73]

At the Synod of Alez in 1620, the French Reformed churches had adopted the Canons of Dordrecht. Diodati, therefore, felt it his duty to urge the Company of Pastors to intervene in the controversy. In fact, in a letter addressed to the Academy of Saumur and dated

November 13, 1635, the Genevan pastors expressed their perplexities about Amyraut, maintaining that in his work they perceived Pelagian tendencies.[74] A more severe judgment was expressed by the Pastors in a document sent to the French Synod of Alençon, convened in 1637 to assess Amyraut's opinions. Diodati was among those who signed the document. In 1639, Diodati was nominated Dean of the Company of Pastors. This was a great honor because the Dean chaired the weekly meetings of the Pastors and represented the Company before the civil authorities of the city.

In 1641, the second edition of Diodati's Italian Bible was published in Geneva.[75] In this edition each book of the Bible was prefaced by a short introduction, and the reader was helped in his reading by the "pious annotations." These were published in English in 1643 under the title *Pious Annotations Upon the Holy Bible: expounding the difficult places thereof Learnedly and Plainly: With other things of great importance. By the Reverend, Learned and Godly Divine, Mr. John Diodati*. The *Annotations* were also translated into German and published for the first time in that language in 1668.[76] The fact that Diodati's *Annotations* were published both in Germany and in England —countries where Bible-reading aids were not lacking—shows how much they and their author were appreciated and valued.

In 1644, *La Sainte Bible interpretée par Jean Diodati* was printed in Geneva. This publication formed the epilogue of a long controversy begun in 1618, when Diodati started to work on his version of the French Bible. His desire to work on a new translation received a great stimulus from the allegations of the Jesuits Veron and Coton concerning the accuracy of the Genevan French Bible. Theodore Tronchin and Benedetto Turrettini were given the responsibility of refuting the claims of the Jesuits. They and the Company of Pastors as a whole took a firm stand on the quality and usefulness of the Bible of the Pastors and Professors of Geneva, published in 1588. Although Diodati did not condemn this translation, he thought it could be improved and that it would have been a mistake to "canonize" a version of the Bible, thereby denying others the freedom to produce new translations.[77] Campi suggests that it is possible to link to this attitude "his exclusion from the group commissioned to defend the validity of the Genevan translations of the Bible."[78]

Because of these convictions, Diodati set to work in order to produce what to his mind was a better translation of the French Bible. But, in 1620, the Synod of Alez expressed a negative opinion about his translation of the Old Testament. Writing after the Synod, Du Mulin asserted that the main reason for the disapproval was that another translation would have given "new reasons to our adversaries to triumph."[79]

Although Diodati's work was rejected, he could not desist from what he perceived to be a work to which he had been called by God. McComish highlights the "deep piety" that led him to undertake his work, and quotes from his letter to the Synod of Alençon: "I shall therefore tell you, That the Providence of God having inclined me in the first years of my Theological Profession, yea, and almost from my very Youth upward, to Translate and Explain the Italian Bible, I was therein so successful...and the greatest Persons in this our Age, had my poor Labours in singular recommendation, which I mention not without blushing; it is the Truth which I publish to the Glory of God only. I was from that very time, excited by a most vehement inward impulse, to Consecrate my Studies wholly unto this self-same Work in two other Languages, the French and Latin."[80]

This dispute proved costly for Diodati. His relationship with many Genevan pastors was damaged, and on several occasions the intervention of the civil authorities was necessary to maintain order and to make sure that satisfactory solutions could be found. In 1638, the translation of the poetical books was published, and, in 1644, Diodati finally received permission to publish the whole Bible at his own expense, a sign of the disapproval of the Company of Pastors. Yet, in spite of all this, he worked during these twenty-six years "with full assurance of innocence, purity and faithfulness...[with] a sure seal of God's calling...[and with] the continuous assistance of his Spirit...."[81] Probably more as a consequence of this controversy within the Company of Pastors than of ill health, Diodati resigned his post at the Academy. He nevertheless continued his pastoral ministry, and was particularly occupied with the attempt to resist the spiritual and moral decline in the city.

His last days were marked by suffering. Beside the estrangement with his colleagues, he experienced health problems and was grieved by the accidental death of his son, Mark. John Diodati died on October 3, 1649. The Genevan pastors recorded that, on October 5, just before his death, he asked Mr. Léger to tell them to watch over the general election. That concern on his deathbed was a spontaneous testimony to a life spent in loving service to the city of Geneva through his work in the Academy and as minister of the gospel. Diodati's influence was to extend all over Europe as well as throughout the English-speaking world through the work of Francis Turretin, one of his students. Turretin is the author of the celebrated *Institutio Theologiae Elencticae*, much of which was translated into English by George Musgrave Giger. The hand-written translation of Turretin's *Institutio* was used as a theological guide for the instruction of students at Princeton Theological Seminary during the time of Charles Hodge, and afterwards at other institutions. The words of Turretin are particularly significant: "To this course (although of my own accord disposed), the domestic example of the two faithful servants of Christ connected with me by blood also impelled me. I mean the great theologian John Diodati, my maternal uncle, whose name (most celebrated through the whole world) and work on the sacred Scriptures (most praised and most worthy of the cedar, to mention no other) demonstrate the illustrious man. Also Benedict Turretin, my most dear parent."[82]

Diodati's life and work have a special place, especially in the hearts of the evangelical people of Italy. His Bible was read in evangelical churches until the beginning of the twentieth century. Even today, the elderly still read Diodati's version, while scholars and pastors quote from it in their studies and sermons. Phillip Mestrezat's words pronounced at Diodati's funeral express the respect of many in Geneva, Italy, and beyond during his lifetime: "A singular gift has been given to us from God: John Diodati, a great man of God and true theologian, already restored and given back."[83]

CHAPTER

2

The Doctrine of Scripture: A Historical Survey

The Bible in the Early Church
The early church emerged at a time when Holy Scripture "already existed as a fact."[84] As has been noted by many scholars, Christ's approach to the Old Testament "forms the strongest possible grounds for the Christian estimate of it, and his approach to his own teaching provides a solid basis for a right assessment of the New Testament."[85] For Christ, the Old Testament Scriptures reflected God's authority (John 10:35; 17:17), and He considered His own teaching as the ultimate and crowning manifestation of that authority (Matt. 5:17, Luke 21:33, John 17:7-8). It is also clear that He esteemed Scripture as authoritative because it was divinely and supernaturally inspired (Matt. 22:43; Mark 12:36).

What was inspired and authoritative for Christ was inspired and authoritative for the Christian church. In the New Testament, a strong belief in the inspiration and authority of Scripture is evident in the attitude of Jesus Himself. As B. B. Warfield put it: "This church-doctrine of inspiration was the Bible doctrine before it was the church-doctrine, and is the church-doctrine only because it is the Bible doctrine.... The church-doctrine of inspiration of the Bible is the Bible's own doctrine of inspiration."[86] The fundamental principle that determined the view of the Bible in the early church was that of the self-authenticating character of Scripture. It is sufficient to quote a few New Testament passages to show that the apostolic doctrine of Scripture reflects that of Christ. The apostle Paul describes the Old Testament Scriptures as "oracles of God" (Rom. 3:2), and declares that "all Scripture is given by inspiration of God" (2 Tim. 3:16).

The apostle Peter has two important passages in his second epistle about the divine nature of both Old Testament and New Testament. He explains that "no prophecy of the scripture is of any private interpretation. For the prophecy came not in old time by the will of man: but holy men of God spake as they were moved by the Holy Ghost" (2 Pet. 1:20-21; cf. Acts 4:25; Heb. 3:7; 9:8; 10:15). Concerning the divine authority of the New Testament, Peter says about Paul's writings: "Even as our beloved brother Paul also according to the wisdom given unto him hath written unto you; as also in all his epistles, speaking in them of these things; in which are some things hard to be understood, which they that are unlearned and unstable wrest, as they do also the other scriptures, unto their own destruction'" (2 Pet. 3:15-16). This statement shows that the early church received the New Testament writings as of equal authority to those of the Old Testament, and although the New Testament does not present a comprehensive and systematic doctrine of Scripture, it does assume and imply one. In fact, the information it provides shows that the early understanding of this doctrine was included in the familiar evangelical theological categories of the clarity, sufficiency, and infallibility of the Bible.[87]

During the second and third centuries, there was a deepening consciousness and a subsequent sharpening of the notion of the Scriptures' authority. This led the Christian church from the middle of the second century to recognize formally the New Testament canon. This process was accelerated by the great struggles against Montanus, Marcion, and the various Gnostic teachers. These challenges did not produce or cause the confessional development of the doctrine of Scripture, but "what did characterize primitive Christianity was a unity of life, of fidelity to the Old Testament, of devotion, and of loyalty to its Lord, as he was witnessed to in the Old and New Testament."[88] For the church, truth was one, and "there could be no pluralism in its confession." This unity centered in Christ "as He was witnessed in the Old and New Testament," and was founded on the belief that the Scriptures were "God-breathed"—that is, "produced by the creative breath of the Almighty."[89] The common belief was that the books of the Bible had been written under the superintendence of the Holy Spirit, and the church fathers were not concerned to investigate deeply the difficult issue of the relationship between the human and the divine in Scripture. There were some—among whom Athenagoras is the best known—who explained the nature of inspiration by means of a tendency to obscure the role of human writers. Athenagoras emphasized the work of the Spirit to such an extent that he affirmed that the prophets acted in a state of ecstasy, so that the Spirit breathed in them "as a musician breathes through a pipe."[90] In general, however, it was not implied that they were purely passive.

It was observed above that the Christ-centered unity that characterized the early church was witnessed "in the Old and New Testament." In addition to drawing attention to the concept of the inspiration of Scriptures, this statement also focuses on the formation of the New Testament canon. In this respect, Marcion of

Sinope was a very important figure. According to Tertullian, "Marcion's special and principal work [was] the separation of the law and the gospel." He presupposed the existence of two gods, "one judicial, harsh, mighty in war, the other mild, placid, and simply good and excellent."[91] The former was the Creator of the world, the God of the Old Testament; the latter was the Father of the Lord Jesus Christ. Because of this difference, Marcion rejected the entire Old Testament, considering it irreconcilable with the New Testament. As a consequence, where the New Testament writings referred to the Old Testament as "Scripture" or employed the formula "It is written," Marcion simply eliminated the passages, thereby taking upon himself the task of expurgating the Scriptures.[92] As a result, Marcion's canon was ultimately composed of part of Luke's Gospel and ten Pauline epistles, and these also were purged of all suspected Old Testament influences.

The German scholar Adolf von Harnack expressed what Pelikan considers to be an "extreme judgment,"[93] namely, that Marcion was the first to compose a formal canon of Christian Scriptures and that the whole church followed his example. Both Pelikan and Metzger quote John Knox's view that Marcion "is primarily responsible for the idea of the New Testament."[94] But when Marcion presented his own canon, formed from the *euangelion* and the *apostolikon*, he was merely revising a list of books currently in use in the church rather than introducing such a list. We should bear in mind that the belief of Christians from the very beginning had been that the church was "built upon the foundation of the apostles and prophets, Jesus Christ himself being the chief corner stone" (Eph. 2:20). Marcion's canon *accelerated* the process of the recognition of the canon by the Christian church, a process already begun in the first half of the second century. He compelled the church to express more clearly what she already believed. A gradual process based on the principle of apostolic transmission of the truth (cf. 1 Cor. 15:1-3) ended in the year 367, when Athanasius declared that only the twenty-seven books of the New Testament as known today were canonical. Although the church of the fathers did not use the term "inerrancy" in relation to these books, they were deeply persuaded that they were free from error.

If Marcion's heresies helped the church to recognize the New Testament canon, Gnosticism and Montanism caused her in the same period to crystallize the idea of the authority and sufficiency of Scripture. Gnosticism, viewed as a chapter in the history of Christian doctrine, may be defined as "a system which taught the cosmic redemption of the spirit through knowledge."[95] Divine mediators, namely Gnostic masters, were the ones who could communicate this *gnosis*; its appropriation was not possible for everyone, but rather only for the *pneumatikoi*, namely, the spiritual men. This redeeming knowledge derived from a special apostolic tradition known and possessed only by Gnostic masters, and was therefore transmitted and received through their own unique succession. Christ's teachings were transmitted not in written form but *viva voce*, and were entrusted to His most faithful disciples. One of the major purposes behind the composition of special Gnostic gospels was that of making known this secret, orally transmitted knowledge.[96] The Gnostics, therefore, opposed their secret tradition to that of the Christian church, received from the apostles.

Montanism was different from Gnosticism in that it did not have its origins in pagan influences and corruptions. Anti-Montanist polemics are notable for the absence of references to mystery religion and cultic aberrations. In Phrygia, Montanus gave impetus to the new movement that was characterized by prophetic ecstasies, viewing it as the religion of the Holy Spirit and the only true form of Christianity. He claimed that his prophecies came directly from "supernatural inspiration by the Holy Spirit."[97] He was assisted by two women—Priscilla and Maximilla—who, having left their husbands, followed the new prophet in his mission.[98] The major emphases of Montanist prophecies were the expectation of the immediate return of Christ and a denunciation of moral laxity. As a consequence, Montanists began to gather and write their prophecies, giving rise to new "holy writings." This presented a great challenge for the Christian church. Indeed, in her reaction to this movement, she became suspicious even of such books as Hebrews and Revelation.

The challenges of both the Montanists and the Gnostics were faced and defeated by the weapon of apostolic authority. The church found her most trustworthy guarantee of the presence and ministry of the Holy Spirit in the authority of the apostles of Christ rather than in the ecstasies of Montanism and in the secret traditions of the Gnostics. Contrary to the most important features of the doctrine of Montanus, to validate her existence "the church looked increasingly not to the future, illuminated by the Lord's return, nor to the present, illuminated by the Spirit's extraordinary gifts, but to the past, illuminated by the composition of the apostolic canon."[99] The promise that the Spirit would lead the disciples into all truth (John 16:13) was understood to mean essentially that the Spirit would lead the apostles into all truth when they wrote the books of the New Testament, and that the whole church would be led into all truth if it was built on their foundation (Eph. 2:20).

The Bible in the Middle Ages

The church fathers devoted all their theological energies to the exposition of some of the central issues of the Christian faith, such as the Trinity, Christology, and soteriology. Having to focus on these controversial topics, they did not develop the doctrine of the inspiration and inerrancy of Scripture, although a high view of Scripture constituted the foundation of all their theological investigation. A definite doctrine of Scripture was to be developed later, in the high scholastic era and during the Reformation and post-Reformation eras. According to Richard Muller, it was not until the late twelfth century that theologians began to inquire into the way in which Scripture is the foundation of the body of Christian doctrine. Despite the absence of an explicit doctrine of *sola Scriptura*, "the declarations concerning the authority, perfection, soteriological necessity, and redemptive sufficiency of Scripture found in medieval theological *systems* provide significant antecedents for the doctrinal declarations concerning Scripture in Protestant scholastic *systems*."[100]

Accordingly, the fundamental issue was not the infallibility and authority of the text, but rather the interpretation of that text. For instance, in discussing the Christological controversies of the first centuries, Pelikan explains that the content of the doctrine of the person of the God-man was supplied by the words and deeds of Jesus Christ and by the witness of all Scripture of Him. He then adds that while all accepted this authority "as set forth in the Bible,"[101] yet there was no common understanding because in order to construct a doctrine of the person of Christ there were variations in the use of Scripture, depending on "differences of opinion about the validity and the limits of allegorical exegesis."[102]

The reason for these hermeneutical difficulties was that, until the fourth century, the opinion prevailed that the oracles of God lay concealed in the Bible under the external forms of the various books. To discover these oracles, therefore, the exegete must penetrate beyond the literal sense. "This conception of Scripture presents a constant inducement to the exegete not to rest content with plain historical typology but to pass over into allegory.... The Scriptures no longer contain 'mysteries' in the New Testament sense of the word: revelations of the purposes of God which were formerly hidden from men's understanding. They *are* mysteries, in the sense of outward forms through which timeless spiritual truths are mediated to the initiate who can perceive them."[103] Moreover, since Christ is the central reference-point of the whole Bible, every single part of it is in principle capable of a Christological interpretation; and because of the connection between Christ and the church, any passage which bears the slightest verbal or conceptual association with Christ or the church may properly be applied to either.[104]

After the struggle between the allegorical school of Alexandria and the more literal school of Antioch, such figures as Jerome, Augustine, and Theodoret of Cyrrhus provided a transition to "an eclectic hermeneutical practice that sometimes emphasized the literal and sometimes the allegorical."[105] Even if at first it seemed that the allegorical school would prevail, ultimately neither the allegorical practices of Alexandria nor the historical emphases of Antioch dominated. By the time of the Chalcedonian era, a more balanced and multifaceted hermeneutic had emerged. Nevertheless, it seems that the dominant orientation of biblical exegesis after this period remained allegorical.[106]

Following the great Trinitarian and Christological controversies, the general atmosphere was determined by the monastic and contemplative ideal rather than by speculative tensions. For this reason, from the seventh century to the eleventh century, the Bible was used to nourish the prayer life of the people, both in private and in public.[107] During this period, it was common to think that spiritual enlightenment belonged not to scholars but rather to the monastic elite. Scholarship and philology could serve only the outward form of the text, while the real spiritual meaning had to be sought at a deeper level. This spiritual meaning was sought in the monasteries through the study of the *sacra pagina* in the pursuit of the *lectio divina*.[108]

One of the major exegetical problems of this period was the notion of multiple senses of Scripture. Origen had established three senses: literal, moral, and spiritual. Gregory the Great also concluded that there were three senses: historical (literal), typological, and moral. The influence of Origen and Gregory prevailed in monasteries because it was more congenial to the nourishment of the spiritual life, while the exegetical methods of Jerome and Augustine, being more literal or historical, predominated later in the schools. To these three traditional senses a fourth was added: the mystagogical or anagogical. After a time of transition, by the middle of the twelfth century, the interpretation of the *sacra pagina* was determined by these four senses. The literal sense exerted no supremacy over the others. In fact, the approach to the text "could result either in a movement from or a gravitation toward the literal sense."[109]

The beginning of the eleventh century ushered in a period that has been variously defined as metaphysical revival, cultural renaissance, or dialectical return.[110] In the monasteries, there was a renewed interest in the scholarly study of the Bible rather than in the mere transmission of past knowledge. This interest took the form of short notes, mostly interwoven with the text or written in the margins, and was brought to its fullest development in the *glossa ordinaria*,[111] which revealed a sober approach to the text designed to remove fanciful interpretations. As time passed, the *glossa* not only provided an explanation of the meaning of the text, but gradually came to include theological *quaestiones* as well, and these were answered by the *disputationis*. It was at this time that the first *Libri Sententiarum* ("Book of Sentences," with a "sentence" being a weighty opinion or statement) began to appear. Anselm of Laon (died in 1117) opened the series of the Books of Sentences, namely, "of collections of texts of the Fathers of the church classified by subject."[112] The master of the Sentences was Peter Lombard. He compiled his Sentences in four books that covered the whole field of theology in a systematic way. It is important to note that the process that led to various compilations of Sentences was exegetical, because these systematic theologies were the end product of a compilation from the *glossa*, the *quaestionis*, and the *disputationes*.[113] Thus, Lombard's collection came to rank as a second text, and lectures were given accordingly both on the Bible and on Lombard's Sentences.

Now the Bible was studied and interpreted to nourish not only piety, but also learning. As in earlier times, the former continued to be cultivated in the monasteries and the latter in the urban schools. The monks pursued the *lectio divina* for the sake of piety; in the schools the scholars pursued the *lectio* for the sake of knowledge. In the schools, an ever-growing confidence in human reason became dominant; strengthened through the *disputationes*, the "supremacy of reason" was claimed over the traditional study of the *sacra pagina*. It was at this time that rationalism as it is known in its modern significance appears.

The effect of the new dialectical climate upon the study of and the approach to the Bible is summarized by Beryl Smalley: "Commentators turned increasingly to philosophy and 'theology': they paid less attention to the Bible in practice, though still regarding it as their primary source in theory."[114] As a result, a preparatory course of instruction was needed in both the monasteries and in the schools, prior to the understanding of biblical studies. This instruction involved grammar, logic, natural science, philosophy, the classics, and even ancient fables about the gods of Greece and Rome. The final death of traditional biblical and theological studies came with Thomas Aquinas (c. 1225-74). By this time, the spiritual senses of Scripture were increasingly reserved for the monastic elite. Aquinas rejected the notion that theology was no more than exegesis with allegorical purpose, and established it as a separate science based on principles of Aristotelian philosophy.[115]

The distinction between the study of the *sacra pagina* and *sacra doctrina* on the one hand, and of *scientia theologiae* on the other, brought about the formulation of at least the basic elements of a doctrine of Scripture. With striking uniformity, the medieval doctors declare the authority of Scripture as the divinely given source of all doctrines of the faith. They deal quite carefully and precisely with the concept of inspiration, recognizing the need to balance the divine and human authorship of the text and, with surprising frequency, noting the relationship between the diversity of genre and literary style within the canon. Aquinas distinguished between various forms of prophecy and between inspiration and revelation. The term "inspiration" indicates that work of the Spirit of God through which the mind acquires the capacity to know divine things, whereas "revelation" points to the communication to man of otherwise inaccessible knowledge. Therefore inspiration can take place independently of revelation, because the mind can be elevated spiritually to a sort of divine wisdom that does not require the impartation of new knowledge.[116] This distinction led Aquinas away from a theory of simple verbal dictation, because inspiration is not impartation of words. Although he could use the traditional metaphor taken from the fathers that the Holy Spirit uses the language of biblical writers as a scribe uses a reed pen, nonetheless, in his opinion, "this is not a process that reduces the human mind to nothing."[117]

On the basis of the statements of Aquinas, Bonaventure, and others in the fourteenth century, the supremacy of the divine authority of Scripture over the insufficiency of human reason to deal with the deep things of God was carried forward. It was Duns Scotus who developed a precise doctrine of Scripture. His reflections about Scripture begin with the assumption that human nature needs the gift of a special doctrine supernaturally inspired, such as cannot be attained by the natural light of the mind. Comparing arguments against the necessity of a revelation from philosophers and arguments in favor of its necessity from Scripture, Scotus concluded that "while the philosophers hold to the perfection of nature and deny supernatural perfection, the theologians truly understand the defect of nature, and the necessity of grace and supernatural perfection."[118] After having argued that natural reason cannot attain to saving truth in the first question of the prologue to his Sentences, Scotus proceeded with a second question, showing that the supernatural knowledge necessary for salvation is sufficiently conveyed in sacred Scripture.

Therefore, as the Middle Ages drew to a close in the fifteenth century, the general persuasion was that the essence of inspiration consisted in the illumination and elevation of the mind of prophets and apostles. This conception would pass over into the sixteenth and seventeenth centuries practically unaffected by revision.

The Bible in the Sixteenth Century
The Renaissance and Humanism

The major contribution of humanism with regard to the doctrine of Scripture is to be found in its literary and philological emphases. In the light of the humanists' watchword *ad fonts* (return to the sources), there was a significant development in the approach to the Bible, characterized by an increased interest in the letter of the text.

This interest was not so much the result of a firm belief that the Scriptures were the Word of God as in the case of the Reformers, but rather was a consequence of the humanists' love for antiquity and eloquence which sprang from their rejection of scholasticism and medieval exegesis.[119] Humanists were convinced that their skill as grammarians and philologists placed them far above the exegetes of the Middle Ages. As a result of this philological passion, there was great progress in the study of Hebrew and Greek, and it was believed that the new techniques of philological and textual analysis proposed by the humanists were the key to enter into the New Testament world and, therefore, into authentic Christianity. For this reason, the biblical erudition of the humanists was considered of such great importance in the struggle to return to the simplicity of the apostolic church.

The influence of Renaissance humanism on John Calvin and on Theodore Beza was to have an effect on their view of Scripture. When Calvin was fourteen, he was sent to Paris by his father to study theology.[120] He began to study philosophy, but after a while he turned to the study of law at Orleans because his father considered that the legal profession would bring financial advantages. There he came strongly under the influence of the humanism affecting the outlook of many teachers in the Universities of France. In 1532, as a consequence of his love for the *bonae litterae*, he published at his own expense a commentary on Seneca's *De Clementia*. Calvin's career as a humanist ended when he became a true Christian. In his own words, "God, by the secret guidance of his providence, at length gave different direction to my course. God by a sudden conversion subdued and brought my mind to a teachable frame. Having thus received some taste and knowledge of true godliness, I was immediately inflamed with so intense a desire to make progress therein, that though I did not altogether leave off other studies, I yet pursued them with less ardour."[121]

Theodore Beza is a very important figure because of his influence in Geneva during the time of Diodati's early life and studies at the Academy. He consolidated what was begun by Calvin and, outliving him by forty-one years, became his theological successor. Beza studied at Orleans and Bourges under his much beloved teacher, Melchor Wolmar, an admirable humanist who instilled a thorough knowledge of both Latin and Greek in his pupils.[122] It was no hyperbole for Beza to claim that there was not a branch of learning into whose mysteries he was not at least partially initiated under the guidance of his instructor.[123] After Wolmar's return to Germany, Beza was sent by his father to study law in Orleans. He found no pleasure in jurisprudence, but poetry attracted him very much. These studies, finished after a period of four years, proved very important to his future as a Reformer. Beza's father wanted his son to immediately begin practicing in the legal profession, but in spite of his station, wealth, and brilliant expectations, the son was happy to dedicate himself to the pursuit of literary studies. His poems, collected early in 1548 under the title of *Juvenalia*, reveal the humanistic character of his education and passions. The fruits of his various studies were to be reaped by Beza throughout his long life. For instance, his Greek editions and Latin translations of the New Testament were basic sources for the Geneva Bible and the King James Version (1611). His *De jure magistratum* (1574), defending the right of revolt against tyranny, grew out of the St. Bartholomew's Day Massacre (1572), from which many surviving French Protestants were welcomed by Beza in Geneva. He overthrew the earlier Calvinist doctrine of obedience to all civil authority, and his book subsequently became a major political manifesto of Calvinism. In 1581, Beza donated to the University of Cambridge the celebrated *Codex Bezae*, an important manuscript from about the fifth century, bearing Greek and Latin texts of the Gospels and Acts, and supplemented by Beza's commentary based on the Calvinist viewpoint. These influences on Calvin and Beza are of fundamental importance with regard to the ethos of the Genevan Academy where Diodati studied under Beza, and where he later taught for many years.

The Reformers and Scripture

The Genevan emphasis on the doctrine of Scripture is of particular significance for an assessment of Diodati's views. In Calvin's *Institutes of the Christian Religion*, the doctrine of Scripture is not dealt with directly, but is rather discussed in the broader context of the subject of the knowledge of God.[124] At the beginning of his *Institutes*, Calvin asserts that man can experience a "twofold knowledge of God" as Creator and Redeemer. [125] In the human mind, by "natural instinct" there is an "awareness of divinity" or "a seed of religion" sown by God Himself.[126] To this revelation of Himself, imprinted in the human heart, God has added another revelation external to man. The final goal of the blessed life, moreover, rests in the knowledge of God. Lest anyone, then, be excluded from access to happiness, God not only sowed in men's minds that seed of religion, but also revealed Himself and still daily discloses Himself in the whole workmanship of the universe.[127] The universe is the "theatre" of God's glory. Yet, in spite of this natural revelation in the soul of man, in creation, and providence, man's receptivity is useless because it has been ruined by sin. Calvin makes reference to the doctrine of sin in its relationship to the innate knowledge of God[128] and to God's external revelation in creation.[129] His conclusion is that "it is needful that another and better help be added to direct us aright to the very Creator of the universe."[130] Calvin finds this better help by acknowledging that God "added the light of his Word by which to become known unto salvation."[131] It is Scripture that, "gathering up the otherwise confused knowledge of God in our minds, having dispersed our dullness, clearly shows us the true God."[132]

At this point, after showing the inadequacy of natural religion and demonstrating that man is thrown back upon the supernatural act of God in communicating His truth to him for any adequate knowledge of God, Calvin's discussion reaches the heart of the question. He holds that the sixty-six books of the canonical Scriptures were handed down in the providence of God in a sound text that meets the test of critical scrutiny. To him, the Bible is the very Word of God. He declares, "We believe that Scripture is from God. It has flowed to us from the very mouth of God by the ministry of men."[133] He considers the doctrine of Scripture in the context of the general topic of the knowledge of God as the power of God "unto salvation," and not as a *locus* in itself. That is why his thinking must be determined by gathering data from the *Institutes* and his commentaries. Speaking of the writers of the Gospels, Calvin says that God "dictated [to them] what they should write."[134] The writers of the Bible "were sure and authentic amanuenses of the

Holy Spirit"[135] that they might consign God's Word "to public records."[136] Calvin comments on 2 Peter 1:20:

> Holy men of God spake as they were moved by the Holy Ghost. They did not of themselves, or according to their own will, foolishly deliver their own inventions. The meaning is, that the beginning of right knowledge is to give that credit to the holy prophets which is due to God. He calls them the holy men of God, because they faithfully executed the office committed to them, having sustained the person of God in their ministrations. He says that they were moved, not that they were bereaved of mind (as the Gentiles imagined their prophets to have been), but because they dared not to announce anything of their own, and obediently followed the Spirit as their guide, who ruled in their mouth as in his own sanctuary.[137]

Considering these statements, Warfield observes that Calvin's language is figurative and that what he has in mind "is not to insist that the mode of inspiration was dictation, but that the result of inspiration is as if it were by dictation, *viz.*, the production of a pure word of God free from all human admixtures."[138] In other words, Calvin's intention is to express the effects rather than the mode of inspiration. In his influential work *The Knowledge of God in Calvin's Theology*, Edward Dowey agrees with Warfield's judgment: "The solution of Warfield, curious as it appears at first glance, is the best formulation for doing justice to a certain lack of clarity or variation in Calvin himself."[139]

Although Theodore Beza was a powerful force in the development and defense of Reformed theology, he wrote no system of doctrine comparable to that of Calvin or to those of later orthodox theologians. This is especially true regarding the doctrine of Scripture. His *Confessio Cristianae Fidei,* published in 1558, and *Quaes-*

tionum et Responsionum Christianarum Libellus of 1570 represent his greatest efforts in the construction of a theological structure. In the *Confessio*, there is no section dealing with the doctrine of Scripture, although in discussing the two parts of the Word of God, the Law and the Gospel, he affirms as follows: "We call Word of God in this matter the canonical books of the Old and New Testament, because they proceed from the mouth of God Himself."[140]

In the *Quaestionum*, the order is God, Scripture, the Trinity, Christ, the application of redemption, faith, justification and sanctification, providence, and predestination, reflecting that of the *Confessio Gallicana* and *Confessio Belgica*, in the formulation of which Beza was personally involved. The *Confessio Gallicana* was prepared by Calvin, and Beza presented it to Charles IX at the religious conference in Poissy in 1561; when it was ratified at the Synod of La Rochelle in 1571, he was the moderator.[141] The second article of the *Confessio Gallicana* states that God reveals Himself to men "in his Word, which was afterward committed to writing in the books which we call the Holy Scriptures," and the fifth article declares that "the Word contained in these books has proceeded from God, and receives its authority from him alone, and not from men."

The *Confessio Belgica* was composed by the martyr Guy de Brès, and Beza himself translated it from French into Latin.[142] Its third article, "Of the Written Word of God," contains the following: "We confess that this Word of God was not sent nor delivered by the will of man, but that holy men of God spake as they were moved by the Holy Ghost, as the apostle Peter saith. And that afterwards God, from a special care which he has for us and our salvation, commanded his servants, the Prophets and Apostles, to commit his revealed Word to writing; and he himself wrote with his own finger the two tables of the law. Therefore we call such writings holy and divine Scripture."

Even though Beza did not write an extensive summary of Christian doctrine nor a lengthy treatise on Scripture, the declarations of these two confessions on the doctrine of Scripture provide a statement of his own view of this doctrine as it is expressed formally, though briefly, in the *Confession* and in the *Quaestionum*.

The Roman Catholic view of Scripture
The development of the Protestant doctrine of Scripture was influenced by internal, positive forces of confessional and doctrinal development as well as external, negative forces of polemic, principally against Roman Catholicism.

The main issue in dispute was the relationship between canonical Scripture and tradition. The Reformers denied that Scripture and tradition are coequal norms, but, on the other hand, held that the superiority of the Word did not imply an automatic rejection of tradition. Their fundamental objection was that the church had promoted the authority of tradition to the same rank as that of Scripture, and ultimately placed it above Scripture insofar as it was its mediator.[143] Therefore, according to the Reformers, God speaks directly to the reader of the Bible without the need of the mediation of the teaching *magisterium* of the church. In the Genevan Confession of 1536, Calvin stated: "We affirm that we desire to follow Scripture alone as the rule of faith and religion, without mixing it with any other thing which might be devised by the opinion of men apart from the Word of God, and without wishing to accept for our spiritual government any other doctrine than what is conveyed to us by the same Word without addition or diminution, according to the command of our Lord."[144]

The Doctrine of Scripture

Therefore, the major problem facing the Reformers was not so much a non-orthodox doctrine of Scripture as this relationship between Scripture and tradition. Whereas the medieval theologians tended to view *sacra theologia* as distinct but inseparable from *sacra pagina*, and universally understood Scripture as the normative foundation for theology, the canon lawyers tended to argue a two-source theory: canon law stands on the two pillars of Scripture and tradition.[145] This was therefore the burning issue for the Christian church in the first half of the sixteenth century: the clash between the principle of *sola scriptura* and the principle of Scripture *and* tradition.[146]

In the light of the challenges presented by the Montanist and the Gnostic heresies that confronted the early church—as the New Testament canon was acknowledged, received, and preserved—it appears that Scripture and tradition coincide with each other. Kelly explains that, during the first four centuries, "Scripture and tradition ranked as complementary authorities, media different in form but coincident in content."[147] The word *tradition* referred simultaneously to the process of communication and to its content.

Heiko Oberman believes that a development of the concept of tradition is to be attributed in the East to Basil the Great (*c.* 330-370).[148] Basil's treatise *On the Holy Spirit* expressed for the first time the idea that the Christian owes equal respect and obedience both to the written and to the unwritten ecclesiastical tradition:

> Of the beliefs and practices preserved in the church, whether by tacit sanction, or by public decree, we have some derived from written teaching; others we have received as delivered to us "in a mystery" from the tradition of the Apostles; *and both classes have the same force* for true piety. If we tried to depreciate the customs lacking written au-

> thority, on the ground that they have but little validity, we should find ourselves unwittingly inflicting vital injury on the Gospel. Dogma and Kerygma are two different things. We keep silent about Dogma: Kerygma is published.[149]

Augustine was later to declare, "For my part, I should not believe the gospel except as moved by the authority of the Catholic Church,"[150] and Roman Catholic theologians argued from Augustine's dictum that *all* authority belonged to the church throughout history, so that she *alone* can prove the validity of the traditions of the apostles, written as well as unwritten.[151] By the time of the Reformation, as movements such as the Waldensians, the Lollards, and the Hussites had already made clear in previous centuries, it was evident to all that the issue at the root of all the others was the doctrine of authority.

In time, this authority became synonymous with infallibility. In the fourteenth century, at the time of the Western Schism and the final phase of the struggle between Pope and Emperor, the canon lawyer was in high demand; if the many bitter comments by doctors of theology are to be believed, he not only equaled but surpassed the theologian in status both at the papal *curia* and the royal courts.[152] It was therefore under the influence of the canon lawyers, who were at work in order to win for Rome the juridical supremacy over all Christendom, that the affirmations of Basil and Augustine acquired the status of a theological argument.

The reaction of the Roman Catholic Church to the position taken by the Reformers was expressed clearly by the deliberations on Scripture of the Council of Trent in April 1546:

> The sacred and holy, oecumenical, and general Synod of Trent,—lawfully assembled in the Holy Ghost, the same three legates of the Apostolic See

presiding therein,—keeping this always in view, that, errors being removed, the purity itself of the gospel be preserved in the church: which (gospel), before promised through the prophets in the holy Scriptures, our Lord Jesus Christ, the Son of God, first promulgated with His own mouth, and then commanded to be preached by His apostles to every creature, as the fountain of all, both saving truth, and moral discipline; and seeing clearly that *this truth and discipline are contained in the written books, and the unwritten traditions* which, received from the Apostles from the mouth of Christ himself, or from the Apostles themselves, the Holy Ghost dictating, have come down even unto us, transmitted as it were from hand to hand: [The Synod] following the examples of the orthodox Fathers, receives and venerates with an equal affection of piety and reverence all the books both of the Old and New Testaments—seeing that one God is the author of both—*as also the said traditions,* as well those appertaining to faith as to morals, as having been dictated, either by Christ's own word of mouth, or by the Holy Ghost, and *preserved in the Catholic Church by a continuous succession.* And it has thought it meet that a list of the sacred books be inserted in this decree....[153] But if any one receive not, as sacred and canonical, the said books entire with all their parts, as they have been used to be read in the Catholic Church, and as they are contained in the old Latin vulgate edition; and *knowingly and deliberately contemn the traditions aforesaid; let him be anathema.* Let all, therefore, understand, in what order, and in what manner, the said Synod, after having laid the foundation of the Confession of faith, will proceed, and what testimonies and authorities it will mainly use in confirming dogmas, and in restoring morals in the Church. Moreover, the same sacred and holy

Synod,—considering that no small utility may accrue to the Church of God, if it be made known which out of all the Latin editions, now in circulation, of the sacred books, is to be held as authentic,—ordains and declares, that the said old and vulgate edition, which, by the lengthened usage of so many ages, has been approved of in the Church, be, in public lectures, disputations, sermons, and expositions, held as authentic; and that no one is to dare, or presume to reject it under any pretext whatever. Furthermore, in order to restrain petulant spirits, it decrees, that *no one*, relying on his own skill, shall,—in matters of faith, and of morals pertaining to the edification of Christian doctrine,—wresting the sacred Scriptures *contrary to that sense which holy mother Church,—whose it is to judge of the true sense and interpretation of the holy Scriptures,—hath held and doth hold*; or even contrary to the unanimous consent of the Fathers; even though such interpretations were never [intended] to be at any time published. Contraveners shall be made known by their Ordinaries, and be punished with the penalties by law established.[154]

What the Council of Trent postulates, therefore, is that not all doctrinal truths are to be found in Holy Scripture. Tradition is seen as a second doctrinal source whose function is not only to unfold the contents of Scripture, but also add to its own substance and complement the content of Scripture.[155]

Conclusion
The above historical survey makes clear that, until the controversy of the sixteenth century on the authority of Scripture and tradition, the church confessed one and the same doctrine about the nature of Scripture. There is a solid continuity between the early church, the medieval church, and the Reformers on this point.

The Doctrine of Scripture

Moreover, in spite of the developments of biblical exegesis as a result of the influence of humanism, the substance of the teaching of the Reformers on the Bible remained basically that of previous centuries. For Calvin and Beza, there was no contradiction or incompatibility between careful philological research and dogmatic theology; rather, it was their exegetical investigations that strengthened their theological commitment. This was therefore the theological line that Diodati naturally followed. He did not introduce anything new in his concept of Scripture, but continued to develop, sharpen, and define the Genevan position on the Bible as the infallible Word of God.

CHAPTER 3

A Translation of Diodati's *Theses theologicae de Sacra Scriptura*

THESIS I

Scriptura Sacra est verbum Dei divinitus inspiratum, et a Prophetis, Apostolis, et Evangelistis in Veteris et Novi Testamenti tabulas, Spiritus Sanctus afflatu relatum, ut inde cognitio omnis ad vitam aeternam necessaria petatur.

Holy Scripture is the divinely inspired word of God, and was brought forth by the Prophets, Apostles, and Evangelists in the books of the Old and New Testament through the breath of the Holy Spirit, so that all knowledge necessary for eternal life may be sought therein.

THESIS II

Scripturae libri vere γνησιοὶ, soli sunt Canonici, ἀναμφελίκτως ὁμολογούμενοι.

The truly authentic books of Scripture are alone canonical, being acknowledged without dispute.

THESIS III

Apocryphi nec parem cum illis auctoritatem sua natura habent, nec aliunde consequi possunt.

The Apocryphal books do not have in their nature equal authority with them, nor can they obtain such authority elsewhere.

Thesis IV

Scripturae editio autentica, ac vere θεόπνευστος, soli sunt fontes Hebraei in Vetere, et Graeci in Novo Testamento.

The authentic text of Scripture, and that which is truly God-breathed, consists only of the Hebrew originals in the Old Testament and Greek originals in the New Testament.

Thesis V

Editio Latina (Vulgatam vocant) est exemplar ἔκτυπον, a quo ad ἀρχέτυπον licet provocare.

The Latin version (they call the Vulgate) is an ectype of the original, from which it is lawful to appeal to the archetype.

Thesis VI

In omnes omnium gentium linguas possunt et debent transferri Scripturae, ut ab omnibus legi possint et intelligi.

Scriptures can and must be translated into all the languages of all nations, so that they may be read and understood by everyone.

Thesis VII

Propter obscuritatem, vel periculum, populum a Scripturae lectione arcere sacrilegum est.

It is a sacrilege to keep people from reading the Scriptures because of obscurity or danger.

Thesis VIII

Obscuritas in Scripturis non tanta est, quin fidei dogmata clare et perspicue sint consignata, et a quovis cum fructu legi possint.

The obscurity in Scripture is not such that the doctrines of faith may not be authenticated clearly and manifestly, and that they [i.e., the Scriptures] are not able to be read with fruit by anyone.

Thesis IX

Periculum in legendis Scripturis, non ab ipsis, sed ab humana temeritate est.

The danger in the reading of the Scriptures is not from themselves, but from human recklessness.

Thesis X

Sensus Scripturae non sunt plures, sed unicus et uniformis, qui ex verborum et sententiarum serie primo et simpliciter Spiritu Sancto propositus animadvertitur.

The meaning of Scripture, originally and plainly intended by the Holy Spirit, is not multiple, but one and uniform, and is understood from the sequence of the words and sentences.

Thesis XI

Allegoria, Anagoge, Tropologia, non sunt Scripturae varii sensus, sed nativi variae applicationes, nec valent ad fidei dogmatum confirmationem.

Allegory, anagogy, and tropology are not varied meanings of Scripture, but varied natural applications, and cannot be used for the establishment of the dogmas of faith.

Thesis XII

Iudex omnis interpretationis est Spiritus Sanctus loquens in Scripturis.

The judge of every interpretation is the Holy Spirit speaking in the Scriptures.

Thesis XIII

Non privati spiritus, quoniam Spiritus Sancti in Scripturis testimonium est publicum.

It is not the testimony of private individuals, since the testimony of the Holy Spirit in the Scriptures is public.

Thesis XIV

Ecclesiae, Conciliis, Doctoribus, et Pastoribus, nullam, nisi ministerialem, interpretandi Scripturam, auctoritatem tribuimus.

We attribute to the Church, Councils, Doctors, and Pastors no authority except the ministerial one of interpreting the Scriptures.

Thesis XV

Regula fidelissima omnis interpretationis, est analogia fidei.

The most faithful rule of every interpretation is the analogy of faith.

Thesis XVI

Scriptura, per et propter se est ἀξιόπιστος, nec Ecclesiae precaria auctoritate indiget.

Scripture is trustworthy by and in virtue of itself, and does not need the precarious authority of the Church.

Thesis XVII

Per et propter se quoque credi a fidelibus asserimus, quod efficit interius Spiritus χρῖσμα et magisterium.

We affirm that by and in virtue of itself it is also believed by believers, because the teaching authority and anointing of the Spirit work inwardly.

Thesis XVIII

Utitur Spiritus Sanctus quibusdam mediis, quibus sese in hominum mentes insinuat: inter haec locum habet Ecclesiae calculus et testimonium.

The Holy Spirit uses certain means, through which He communicates Himself into the minds of men: among these [means], the decision and witness of the Church have a place.

Thesis XIX

Per Ecclesiam credi potest, propter Ecclesiam credere non est fides.

[A teaching] can be believed through the Church, [but] to believe because of the Church is not faith.

Thesis XX

Scriptura omnia perfectissime continet ad salutem necessaria.

Scripture contains most completely all things necessary for salvation.

Thesis XXI

Necessaria ergo Scriptura, quia ea aliunde peti non possunt.

Scripture is therefore necessary, because those things cannot be sought elsewhere.

Thesis XXII

Scripturas solum de bene esse (ut loquuntur) Ecclesiae dicere impium est.

To say that the Scriptures are only for the well being of the Church (as they say) is ungodly.

Thesis XXIII

Traditiones non scriptae non sunt ad salutem necessariae: vel enim pro nullis habendae, vel sunt mutabiles, quia ad πολιτείαν Ecclesiae solum spectant.

Unwritten traditions are not necessary for salvation: for they either must be considered of no value, or they are mutable, for they concern only church polity.

Thesis XXIV

Pontificias Traditiones esse vel Christi vel Apostolorum negamus.

We deny that the pontifical traditions are either from Christ or from the Apostles.

Thesis XXV

Haec contra Pontificios, contra Libertinos et Enthusiastas asserimus, spiritus omnes ex Scripturis probandos; ipsumque adeo Spiritum Sanctum Scripturae examen non refugere.

These things we assert against the Pontiffs, against the Libertines and against the Enthusiasts, testing all the spirits by the Scriptures, since the Holy Spirit Himself does not flee from the test of Scripture.

CHAPTER

4

Diodati's Doctrine of Scripture in his *Theses theologicae de Sacra Scriptura*

A theological and historical commentary, with additional reference to Diodati's *Pious Annotations upon the Holy Bible*

This chapter aims to explain Diodati's understanding of the doctrine of Scripture in the context of the theological controversies and the historical circumstances of his day. This analysis will discuss the factors that shaped Diodati's theses with the goal of shedding light on the historical development of the Protestant view of Scripture.

Comment on Thesis I

Diodati commences the discussion of his thesis by asserting the divine origin of the Scriptures as follows: "Holy Scripture is the divinely inspired word of God," in the sense that it comes by "the breath of the Holy Spirit." This language reflects the concept of "the creative breath of God," which is deeply rooted in the Hebrew mind. The expression "the breath of the Almighty" (cf. Job 32:8; 33:4) was a traditional Hebrew way of describing the creative act of God and, as Warfield pointed out, "it is indeed the whole conception of the Spirit of God as the executive of the Godhead that is involved here: the conception that it is the Spirit of God that is the active agent in the production of all that is."[156]

In articulating this concept, Diodati's student Jaques Duchat affirmed in 1620, in his fourth thesis on *de Verbo Dei*, that "the efficient cause of Holy Scripture is God the Father, in the Son, through the Holy Spirit."[157] In his *Pious Annotations upon the Holy Bible*, Diodati comments on Genesis 1:2 thus: "*The Spirit]* that is, the third Person of the most holy Trinity, immediately and through its proper operation: which is to preserve, and maintain all things in their being, which they have received by the supreme will of the Father, and the productive action of the Son."[158] On Genesis 2:7, speaking of the creation of the soul of man through the divine "breathing," he explains that this was accomplished by "virtue proceeding immediately from God, to create the soul of man." Reflecting on Psalm 33:6, Diodati says that the heavens were made "by sending forth and bringing to pass his will and efficacious decree." Then he adds: "*By the breath*] viz. by his word and command. Or, by the subsisting Spirit, which is the third person in Trinity, inseparable from the other two, as well in essence as in operation, Gen. 1:2, Job 33:4."

Applying this concept to the doctrine of Scripture, it is the Spirit who breathed into existence the words of Scripture because God's chosen servants had, as they were moved by the Spirit, "the gift of His [God's] presence and infallible inspiration."[159] For Diodati, therefore, the Scriptures are divinely inspired because they are the result of the creative breathing of God through the work of the third person of the Trinity (although in his comments on such passages as 2 Timothy 3:16 and 2 Peter 1:19-21, he does not give detailed attention to this theme).

After establishing the divine source of the Scriptures, Diodati is careful to explain that what is "brought forth by the Prophets, Apostles, and Evangelists" is to be attributed to the special inspiration of God's Spirit. This order, typical of Reformed orthodoxy, presupposes two efficient causes: *auctor* and *ministri illius*.[160] Duchat's thesis therefore affirms that "the title [*sacras Literas*] is taken in part from God's Spirit dictating through his amanuenses, prophets and apostles, in part from the efficient, material, formal, and final causes,"[161] and he develops his assertion further by saying that "the instruments used to reveal the Word have been now Patriarchs, now Prophets, now Apostles."[162]

In common with previous Reformers and theologians, Diodati makes little effort in his *Annotations* to substantiate and analyze the concept of the divine inspiration of the human writers of the Bible, especially the relationship between the dictating and the amanuenses. As a result, there is a tendency to think that the teachings of people like Luther, Calvin, Diodati, and other divines on this issue seem contradictory or, at best, unclear. The reason for this lack of emphasis, however, is that this relationship was not a matter of dispute with Roman Catholicism. As noted above, Diodati does not even mention the divine inspiration of the human writers when commenting on 2 Timothy 3:16. On John 10:35, he simply affirms that Scripture cannot be broken in the sense that it cannot be "gainsaid, refuted, and reproved as false." Writing on 2 Peter 1:11 about the "spirit of Christ" who was in the prophets of old, he says merely that the apostle is speaking about "that Spirit by which all the prophets were inspired and have spoken, which proceeds from the Father, and the Son."

It seems that the most important issue for Diodati was not to explain the mechanisms of inspiration and the modalities that regulated the relationship between divine and human wills, but rather the fact that inspiration "belongs to the production of the canonical

Scriptures and not to either the apocrypha or to the writings of the church's postbiblical tradition."[163]

Regarding the purpose of the Scriptures, Diodati shows that they have been given so that from them may be derived "all knowledge necessary for eternal life."[164] In his *Annotations* on Romans 1:18, he speaks of man's condition before God as follows: "Being in servitude and bondage to their own perversity and malice, by which they hinder the truth from having dominion over their actions. *The truth*] namely all that light, knowledge of God and of his nature, judgment, and will, as hath remained in them after sin, v. 25." According to Diodati, the apostle "proveth that there is yet some truth, that is to say, some knowledge of God in man after sin," but men "lost all manner of truth, of understanding, all pureness of judgment, and true aim, forsaking voluntarily the guide of that light, especially in matters concerning God's service and true Religion."[165] Considering Paul's declaration that "the world by wisdom knew not God" (1 Cor. 1:21), Diodati says, "Namely, in the frame and Table of this world, which represents the infinite wisdom of God in its creation and conduct. *By wisdom*] namely, by the right use of reason and discourse." It is clear then that Diodati, following the classic Genevan formulation, considers the Scriptures as the *principium cognoscendi theologiae* (the chief means by which God is known).

The Scriptures are the source of the true knowledge of God because of the sinful condition of man. God has given His Word so that man might receive the knowledge necessary to obtain eternal life. Sin has not only placed man in perdition, but has also taken from him the capacity to understand his condition before God in order to find a way of escape. God has therefore provided another source of revelation—a special revelation —so that man might receive the essential knowledge of

God and the way of salvation. On Psalm 19, Diodati makes the following comments concerning the Word of God spoken of in verse 7: "*Is perfect*] it seems that this perfection is contrary to the line which is spoken of before, namely, a rough and imperfect revelation by means of the creatures, which declare but obscurely some generality of God's nature, whereas the Word reveals at full, both His nature and His will, as far as is necessary for man's salvation." Diodati repeats the same concepts in commenting on Romans 10:17: "*By hearing*] That is to say, it is not grounded, nor doth resolve itself into natural principles, nor into discourse of reason, nor into human authority, nor into apprehension of the understanding, but only into the declaration which is made thereof to man: which also hath neither truth, nor power, but only by its faithful relation and conformity to God's original word." Therefore, says Duchat, "since truly the working of nature, though admirable in regard to the knowledge of the perfect will of God, is not enough, let us take refuge in the Holy Writings."[166]

Comment on Thesis II
After discussing the nature and purpose of Scripture, Diodati proceeds by identifying what should be regarded as Scripture. He does so first of all in positive terms, showing that "the truly authentic books of Scripture are alone canonical, being acknowledged without dispute." Diodati speaks of the "books" that are to be regarded as "Scripture," emphasizing that the Word of God is a revelation committed to writing. As his thesis was to be discussed at the end of the three years' curriculum of studies at the Academy of Geneva, Diodati's language is succinct. It is obvious that, for him, the books are those of the Old and New Testaments, as they are recorded in the French and Belgic Confessions.

At this point in the development of his discussion, Diodati's interest lies in distinguishing the books that are canonical from those that are not. He is preparing to refute all the incongruities of the Roman Catholic doctrine of Scripture while, at the same time, establishing the Reformed view. This interest sprang from what might be described as pastoral concern of Protestant orthodoxy, rather than from a detached and merely speculative dogmatizing. His deep concern for the welfare of the churches and of the cause of the Reformation in Italy has been mentioned in Chapter 1; the practical and pastoral ends stated in theses VI and VII, to be discussed later, confirm this observation.

But why is it so important for Diodati to identify the books that are canonical? What is at stake? According to the usage of the ecclesiastical writers of the first three centuries, the word κανών (canon) indicates what was normative in matters of belief in the churches. Later, beginning in the fourth century, the term began to be used to signify the writings of the Old and New Testaments.[167] This understanding remained virtually unchanged up to the time of the Reformation. The Protestant position on the identity of the canon was determined by the controversy with Roman Catholic theologians and was concerned essentially with the matter of authority.

The Reformation saw the application of the *sola Scriptura* principle as the non-negotiable rule for all other grounds of authority. The focus of the exposition of the Protestant doctrine of Scripture "is clearly the character of Scripture as rule or norm and the way in which Scripture ought to be considered as prior to the church and its traditions."[168] Because Diodati regarded the canon as the *regula fidei*, it was crucial for him to identify it clearly and precisely.

Comment on Thesis III

This thesis is a negative statement about the identity of the Scriptures, and constitutes the logical conclusion of the discussion begun in Thesis II. In his fascinating analysis of the debate over the canon, Richard Muller explains that, because of the threat posed by the Marcionites and the Gnostics, the early church developed an adequate concept of the canon of the New Testament, but "it had not provided a definitive listing of the doctrinally normative books of the Bible."[169] In *De Doctrina Christiana*, Augustine acknowledged what came to be generally recognized as the contents of the New Testament, although the books have a different order. He then added the following guidelines:

> Accordingly, among the canonical Scriptures he will judge according to the following standard: to prefer those that are received by all the catholic churches to those which some do not receive. Among those, again, which are not received by all, he will prefer such as have the sanction of the greater number and those of greater authority, to such as are held by the smaller number and those of less authority. If, however, he shall find that some books are held by the greater number of churches, and others by the churches of greater authority (though this is not a very likely thing to happen), I think that in such a case the authority on the two sides is to be looked upon as equal.[170]

It is clear that, in spite of the influence of such leaders as Augustine, a measure of disagreement about the canon remained in the sixteenth century. But what caused this partial disagreement to cease in the sixteenth century? In Muller's words,

> Absolute closure of the canon and its integral perfection were issues that came to be of doctrinal

importance only when the bounds of the canon and its relation to the authoritative tradition and magisterium of the church became a matter of faith —a confessional or creedal issue.... The starting point of debate, then, for the theologians of the second generation of the Reformation and early Protestant orthodoxy was the teaching of the Council of Trent expounded at the fourth session of the council on 8 April 1546.... Trent offered, *for the first time in the history of the church*, an absolutely clear and determinate canon—and offered it, on the authority of the church, as a matter of the faith.[171]

In response to the attacks of the Reformers, the first task of the Council of Trent was "to delimit the spheres of Scripture and Tradition."[172] The decree of the fourth session concerning the canonical Scriptures was based on tradition, and the Council, by pronouncing an *anathema* in the decree, was requiring that its teaching be accepted because it came from the church. Calvin recognized the fundamental theological problem regarding the Roman Catholic version of the canon: "A most pernicious error widely prevails that Scripture has only so much weight as is conceded to it by the consent of the church.... What reverence is due Scripture and what books ought to be reckoned within its canon depend, they say, upon the determination of the church."[173] The French and Belgic Confessions, in the formulation of which Beza had such a significant role, deny that the canonical books receive their authority from the church and that the Apocrypha has legitimacy as a basis for any articles of faith. This was exactly the position of Diodati.

In his *Annotations*, he provides an "advertisement concerning the Books, which are called *Apocrypha*" between the Old and New Testaments. He writes:

> There was a Register or authentic Catalogue made of all the said Books, gathered into one volume by *Ezra*.... This volume being gathered together, was the firm rule of the Church at that time, the only model of all its Religion and divine worship: the foundation of all their hopes, the form and sovereign Law of their customs and government; and the only subject of all their expositions and Lectures, which were made in their Assemblies. And though there were even at that time, many other books of pious subjects...yet the Jewish Church never gave place for public uses to any other books, but such as were truly divine and sacred, and comprehended within their Catalogue. The same care of the divine providence was also showed in the Christian Church.... But the Christian Church after the death of the Apostles, did not use the same scrupulous circumspection as the Jewish Church did: for many writings of seeming piety, passing through the Church's hands, under the name of divine books; the care and severity in discerning them, and cutting off the supposed ones, was not used.... Neither the Lord, nor the holy Apostles have ever honored or authorized them, by alleging any of them, as they have done the most part of the other true authentic books.... In conclusion, they may be read, and good instruction may be gathered out of them...applying always the rule of God's authentic Word thereunto, and the light of his Spirit, to discern truth from falsehood, and good from evil; and to retain the one, and reject the other: according to the liberty which believers have in all works and writings, which are merely human.[174]

It is now clear why Diodati declares that the books of the Apocrypha "do not have in their nature equal authority with them [the canonical books], nor can they obtain such authority elsewhere."

Comment on Theses IV and V
Diodati develops his discourse by concentrating next on the issue of the authentic edition of the text of Scriptures. He affirms that the "the authentic text of Scripture, and that which is truly God-breathed, consists only of the Hebrew originals in the Old Testament and Greek originals in the New Testament." Having given attention to the problem of the canon itself, Diodati now considers the issue of the various books that form the canon. "With the canon settled, next came the question of the text."[175]

At this point in his life and work, Diodati is more concerned with the edition of the text than with the question of its integrity. Even later in his life, he does not seem to have been influenced by the polemics concerning textual problems much debated in the seventeenth century.[176] Milka Ventura offers the following opinion:

> As to the problem of the vowel-text and the other philological issues debated in his time, Diodati's attitude does not seem much influenced by the controversy that opposed the school of Saumur to the more conservative theologians.... It seems that Diodati is influenced more . . . by the complexities that were debated at the turn of the century, when he was being formed under the guidance of Casaubon and Theodore de Beza, rather than by those of the late sixteenth century.[177]

This observation implies that, in the development of his argument, Diodati is thinking first and foremost of the Council of Trent's position on the doctrine of Scripture, and the relationship between that doctrine and the role of tradition in the church and with its magisterium. This supposition is confirmed by Thesis V, which specifies the Reformed position on the place and authority of the Vulgate: "The Latin version (they call the Vulgate) is an ectype of the original, from which it is lawful to appeal to the archetype."

In the fourth session at Trent, the Council made the following statement:

> The same sacred and holy Synod . . . ordains and declares, that the said old and Vulgate edition, which, by the lengthened usage of so many ages, has been approved of in the Church, *be, in public lectures, disputations, sermons, and expositions, held as authentic*; and that no one is to dare, or presume to reject it under any pretext whatever.[178]

Muller observes that the decree is carefully worded "and in no way argues an absolute priority of the Vulgate as a translation over the Greek and Hebrew text, but it does define the authority of the Vulgate in such a way that none of its renditions of the original languages could be superseded as norms for theological statement."[179] At the end of the fifteenth and sixteenth century there was a certain degree of agreement about the need to make reference to the Hebrew and Greek originals of Scripture; but, as the theological storm became more and more severe, the version of the Bible used to settle disputes turned out to be of great importance.

"But what exactly did the Council mean by declaring the Vulgate authentic?" asks F. J. Crehan. He supplies the answer to his own question: "It should first be noted what the decree omitted to say. It did not say that the Vulgate was by Jerome nor distinguish it from the Old Latin; it did not call for its revision; it did not say what its relation was to the original Greek and Hebrew texts. The sense of the declaration was to make the Vulgate a reliable source of dogmatic arguments for theological teaching and debate." And then he adds an important observation: "The ground of this reliability was not its relation to the originals, close or otherwise, but the fact that it had been for so many centuries in constant use for this purpose by the Church, which could not have used it for so long without engaging thereby its supreme teaching authority."[180]

As for Diodati, there is much evidence that his attitude toward the Vulgate was not determined by a blind and bigoted hatred of Catholicism and its theologians. In her research, Milka Ventura has a lengthy section of about 100 pages on the sources that Diodati used in his work as translator of the Bible, and there is an important sub-section devoted to Diodati's relationship with the Vulgate.[181] Diodati shows great respect for Jerome, and is much influenced by him as a translator. In a letter written to the Synod of Alençon in 1637, Diodati mentions his admiration for Jerome.[182] Diodati explains that he followed Jerome where he could do so "with a safe conscience." In practice, this means that Diodati generally followed Jerome, taking a different position only when the Roman Catholic theological stance made appeal to some passages in the Vulgate wrongly or imperfectly translated.

Diodati's attitude towards Jerome highlights the real issue: the theological implications of the primacy of the Vulgate in public lectures, disputations, sermons, and expositions when solving of doctrinal controversies. Francis Turretin, who studied theology under Diodati, is very straightforward in his explanation: "The question is, have the original texts (or the Hebrew and Greek manuscripts) been so corrupted either by copyists through carelessness (or by the Jews and heretics through malice) that they can no longer be regarded as the judge of controversies and the rule to which all the versions must be applied? The papists affirm, we deny it."[183]

The protest of the Reformers had been directed against many issues, all springing from the peculiar view of the tradition of the Church of Rome. For instance, the Vulgate translated "it shall bruise thy head" in Genesis 3:15 as *"ipsa* conteret caput tuum" (emphasis added), using the feminine pronoun and rendering this verse a Mariological proof text. Another passage used to justify the cult of Mary was Luke 1:28: "And the angel came in unto her, and said, Hail, thou that art highly favoured, the Lord *is* with thee: blessed art thou among women," rendered by the Vulgate "et ingressus angelus ad eam, dixit ave *gratiai plenai* Dominus tecum benedicta tu in mulieribus" (emphasis added). In this case, the fault is not so much with Jerome—though in his translation he does not render the passive—as with the interpretation of the Roman Church. Another concern of the Reformers was those passages from the Vulgate used to support the sacramental system. One of the most famous was Matthew 4:17, where the imperative "Repent" is translated *"paenitentiam agite,"* namely, "do penance." These few examples are enough to indicate what was the real issue at stake.

It is important to add that when Diodati speaks of the "Hebrew originals in the Old Testament and Greek originals in the New Testament," he is not referring to the *autographa*, but to the *apographa*.[184] With regard to the purity of the text, Francis Turretin makes the following relevant comment: "By the original texts, we do not mean the *autographs* written by the hand of Moses, of the prophets and of the apostles, which certainly do not now exist. We mean their *apographs* which are so called because they set forth to us the word of God in the very words of those who wrote under the immediate inspiration of the Holy Spirit."[185]

These two theses demonstrate that Diodati is not yet concerned with the issues raised in the second half of the sixteenth century by the critical study of the text of the Bible, and used by Socinians, Deists, Rationalists, and Arians as a weapon against the fundamental articles of the Christian faith. Rather, his concern is to refute the claim of the Papists for the superiority of tradition and the magisterium of the church over the Bible.

Comment on Thesis VI
The declaration of Thesis VI concerning the translation of the Scriptures "into all the languages of all nations" expounds the central issue of Diodati's life, thought, and career. The work of translating Scripture was, to him, a divine calling. As he himself explained in a letter to Jacques Auguste de Thou, he had begun the great labor of the translation of the Italian Bible in his "first youth," with "utmost care," with "all the powers," and with "the most careful conscience" of which he was able.[186] After that work, Diodati affirms that he was "from that very time, excited by a most vehement inward impulse" to consecrate his studies "wholly unto this self-same Work in two other Languages, the *French* and *Latin*."[187] At the heart of Diodati's work there is a deep, theological conviction that the purpose of the Scriptures is to impart "all necessary knowledge for eternal life." In fact, in the above-mentioned letter to de Thou, Diodati explains that he was moved by the desire "to open to our Italians the door of the knowledge of celestial truth." Therefore, as is clear from the terminology used by Diodati, he considered the work of translating the Bible a means to bring people to a saving knowledge of the gospel, and accordingly he declares that "many persons owed their Illuminations, and sincere Conversions" to the Italian Bible.[188]

In order to gain an adequate understanding of Diodati's view of the importance of translating the Bible into vernacular languages, we must turn our attention to his work on the French version of the Bible. His Italian version had been well received; after the first edition in 1607, it was revised and reprinted in 1641, mainly to improve the style. Concerning his translation of the Bible in Italian, Diodati could render the following testimony to the Synod of Alençon:

> The Providence of God having inclined me in the first years of my Theological Profession; yea, and almost from my very Youth upward, to Translate and Explain the *Italian* Bible, I was therein so successful, and the Blessing of God did so wonderfully follow me in it, that both *Jews* and *Christians*; yea, those of the *Romish Church* also, and others of all Professions, conceived a very great esteem for me, and the greatest Persons of this our Age, had my Poor Labours in singular recommendation, which I mention not without blushing; it is the Truth which I publish to the Glory of God only.[189]

There are no reasons to doubt this assertion. Indeed, even Diodati's enemies recognized the value of his work. In 1644, Cardinal Antonio Barberini wrote from Rome in alarm to the Inquisitor of Florence ordering him to endeavor to prevent Diodati's Bible from entering Italy. Barberini said, "The ministers of the city of Geneva are always meditating to introduce in Italy scriptures full of the poison of their perfidious heresies, and trying insidiously to insert them in the versions of holy scripture, captivating the simple people as well as the more intelligent *with refinement of style and clarity of version.*"[190] McComish acknowledges that "Diodati's achievement was to produce, single handed, one of the main Bibles of European protestantism," and that his work "stands on a level with that of the Luther Bible in German and the Authorized King James' Bible in English."[191]

On the other hand, the publication of Diodati's French version of the Bible encountered many obstacles.

As explained in the first chapter, these obstacles caused him deep sorrow.[192] At the same time, they also gave him an opportunity to explain his reasons, his aims, and the principles and methods he followed in his work of translation. It is important to note again the words of McComish: "The controversy revealed the man. The struggle to publish the French Bible revealed the complete dedication of Giovanni Diodati to his self-appointed task."[193]

After many unsuccessful endeavors to obtain official permission to publish his French translation, Diodati fully expresses his ideas on the problem of translating the Bible into the vernacular in his appeal to the Synod of Alençon of 1637. In the introductory part of his letter, Diodati tries to make clear the providences, the sentiments, and the aims that led him in his work. He is convinced that a new French Bible was a necessity "acknowledged by the National Synod held at *Montauban*, in the year 1590 and afterward, by very many Persons of Note and Quality."[194] Concerning his motivation, Diodati writes:

> I should be too tedious and troublesome, most Honored and Dear Brethren, if that by many words I should go about to persuade you to believe, that either Avarice or Covetousness, moved me to undertake this Vast and Laborious Work, or love of Novelty, or affectation of Singularity, much less had that black and malignant Vice any Influence or Power over me, *viz.* to Eclipse and Darken the Glory of our Renowned Fathers in the Reformation, and to arrogate it wholly to my self. I am at this time of the day too near the direct line of the Sun, and so disabled from ever casting any great Shadows, or to be wrapped up in such thick Mists.... I have Labored without Wages, I have Wrought without any Thanks or Favor, my Works

have not gotten me any Honor. I aimed only at this mark, to make clear and limpid this Fountain of Life; my design was to help poor and needy Souls to drink largely and comfortably of it, and to make the way to Salvation plain and easy unto all; and to gather up the stones out of the Lord's Field, out of the Churches Heritage, and to cleanse the Lamps of this Golden Candlestick, and to render this strong Meat pleasant to the taste, delightful, and easy of digestion; and to consecrate this Heavenly *Manna* in its pot of Gold.... I have Labored to free the reading of the Holy Scriptures from certain and yet very common abuses...I have endeavored to make it plain and easy to the simple.[195]

After these introductory remarks, Diodati states the reasons that moved him and that, therefore, justify his work. First, he affirms that "it hath been the constant practice of all Ages from the very birth of Christianity, that all Nations and Languages have not only suffered, but even carefully Collected and Embraced a Diversity of Translations of the Holy Scripture."[196] Secondly, he states that the work of Bible translation is a "liberty" that did not cause "considerable inconvenience"; rather, time has "suppressed the vicious and ill performed, and given Authority unto good Translations."[197] Thirdly, Diodati appeals to the mandate of Calvin himself and of "those of the year 1588," saying that, in the preface to the Bible of the Genevan Company of Pastors, they "never designed by their performances, to exclude and debar any of their Successors from attempting such a Work as this; but rather did invite, exhort, and summon them to contribute what should be in their power for the perfection of that, which according to their Candor and Modesty they said, they had left imperfect."[198] Further, he explains the necessity of his work because of the changes that occur in human languages. These changes caused some "Words, Terms and Phrases as were seemly and sounded well in one Age, yet in the next following hear ill, are barbarous, putrid, and intolerable."[199] Another reason is that those who interpret a text of the Bible in order to explain and teach it to others have "the privilege to translate the Letter of the Text" before giving their own comments.[200]

Diodati's sixth motivation shows much humility. Since "in all Times and Languages there have been Translations of the Bible for publick use Authorised by the common Magistrate...and of others for private use only," he would be content if his French version would "be confined to this lower Classes and Condition." Then he added, even more specifically, "Without any complaint of mine, or of any one for me."[201] The seventh reason is the necessity to "give place to the obligations of Conscience." The "only mark" at which Diodati aimed was "the removing of Stumbling-blocks from the blind and the weak, excuses from the lazy, occasions from the Adversary, and the hindrances of profiting in the knowledge of the Holy Scriptures from all." This aim, he believed, reflected the divine purpose in the giving of Scripture: "Because all Sacred Scripture is Divinely inspired for these very ends and purposes."[202]

Diodati has been moved also by the expediency of this liberty for fear that "the singularity of one Translation always heard, read, and handled publicly and privately, should come at length to be Canonized." He then explains that this is what happened in the Church of Rome, that "not at first by any public Declarations, but by custom, and length of time the Vulgar *Latin* hath obtained this Reputation."[203]

The ninth reason given is a plea to the Synod to be sensitive and considerate towards himself: "We ought to be very careful by my example, of abating their courage, who have the Gift and Will to employ themselves in this kind of Study, for fear lest they should toil and labor in vain, which is the highway leading unto despair." Moreover, Diodati calls the Synod to soberness and humility: "And a Very foolish Opinion it is, to think, that we are come to such a pitch of perfection, as if nothing among us could be bettered."[204] In the tenth argument, he affirms that "the permitting of Translations done by Faithful and Approved hands, is so far from increasing, as is pretended, an endless number of them, that on the contrary, it is the true means to obstruct and prevent it: for at last there shall come forth one which will give the stunning blow unto all the rest, as that of St. Hierom's did."[205] The last justification is that, as it is useful to maintain liberty to explain certain passages unessential to the Reformed cause in sermons and lectures, so there should be the same freedom in the translation of the Bible, "lest being too much captivated by one Translation, we should at last meet with all those Defects, Obscurities, and Wanderings from the Scripture-Sense, and take upon us to forge Mysteries at our own wills, which we have justly condemned in the *Church of Rome.*"[206]

If Diodati's French Bible was prevented from becoming one of the main vernacular versions in French because of the controversy within the Genevan Company of Pastors and the school of Saumur, his Italian Bible has known great popularity for more than three centuries. Throughout the seventeenth and eighteenth centuries, it was frequently reprinted; the reprints were printed outside Italy because of the persecution of Italian Protestants. It was reprinted in 1665 in Holland, and many times in the eighteenth century in Germany: in 1702 in Liepzig, in 1711 in Nuremberg, in 1712 in Cologne, again in Liepzig in 1744, and in Dresden in 1757. In 1808, the New Testament was published for the first time in London under the auspices of the

British and Foreign Bible Society, the first of many printings in England.

During the Italian Unification, when Italy was undergoing a process of social and religious renewal that would culminate with the end of the Pontifical State in 1870, Diodati's Bible knew unprecedented popularity.[207] In those decades, it became a symbol of religious and civil freedom. The only version previously allowed in Italy was the Vulgate; as a result, only those people who knew Latin could read the Bible. The colporteurs of the Bible Society followed Garibaldi's soldiers, and when the "Thousand" liberated Sicily in 1860, a Bible depot was opened in Palermo. When Garibaldi's militia reached Naples many street merchants begun to shout "The Book, the Book!" as they were distributing Diodati's Bible.

Comment on Thesis VII
In a book published in 1997 and related to the "Year of the Bible" promoted by the Italian bishops of the Roman Catholic Church, Gigliola Fragnito observes that Italians' lack of familiarity with the Bible is not a consequence of secularization, but "as a matter of fact, it is the result of a kind of abolition imposed by Rome for more than two centuries by the prohibition of the reading of Italian translations."[208] This prohibition was the response of the Church of Rome to Europeans' increasing sense of the necessity for a church reformation, beginning in the eleventh century and culminating in the Protestant Reformation. Indeed, it was a deep conviction of the Congregation of Inquisition that the propagation of the Protestant heresy was directly attributable to the vernacular Bibles.

In the second half of the twelfth century, when the vernacular languages of Europe were freeing themselves from the supremacy of Latin, Waldo of Lyons paid some clergy to translate parts of the Bible from the Vulgate. They prepared a "Bible-anthology" for Waldo, adding exegetical comments by the ancient fathers.[209] This is one of the earliest examples of the progressive diffusion in the late Middle Ages of reading the Bible in vernacular.[210] Throughout Europe, the religious impulse coming from what the Church of Rome considered heretical movements aroused a popular interest in the Bible. Previously, the Bible was a book only for scholars, but the corruption of the clergy and the practical denial of the gospel of Christ by the conduct of those who stood before the people as the visible representation of Christianity created a growing aspiration towards a reformation and therefore towards reading the sacred text of Christianity. This aspiration caused many common people, such as Waldo, to become deeply interested in the message of the Bible. In the fifteenth century, just before the Reformation, vernacular versions of the Bible were available in many places in Europe, although in many cases they were not complete translations.

Until the time of the Reformation, the Church of Rome had been able to keep control over popular movements that yearned for a religious renewal of the church. Sometimes they were absorbed back into the structure of Roman Catholicism; in other cases, when they refused to compromise and submit to the power of Rome, they were repressed by violence.[211] For this reason, the prohibitions of the vernacular Bibles had been local and confined. Only with the Reformation did the Church of Rome, losing her power in much of Europe, have to take a stand on the issue of the translation of the Bible. The trouble for Rome was that the availability of the Scriptures to the common people was a threat to the theory of *duo genera christianorum*—that is, the distinction between clergy and laity as the foundation of the magisterium of the church, and therefore to her authority. As a result, Rome developed the argument that, "because of obscurity or danger," people had to be kept from reading Scripture apart from the guidance of the church. This argument for Diodati was "sacrilege."

That the issue of vernacular Bibles was a matter of authority is evident from a resolution against the Wycliffites:

> We resolve therefore and ordain that no one henceforth *on his own authority* translate any text of Holy Scripture into the English or any other language by way of a book, pamphlet or tract, and that no book, pamphlet or tract of this kind, whether already recently composed in the time of the said John Wyclif or since, or to be composed in the future, be read in part or in whole, publicly or privately, under pain of the greater excommunication, until the translation shall have been approved by the diocesan of the place, or if need be by a provincial council.[212]

The essential issue that Diodati is trying to face in Thesis VII, therefore, Roman Catholicism's claim, pursued since the beginnings of the heretical movements in the Middle Ages, that the church has the office of "mediation" between the Scripture and the believer.

Comment on Theses VIII and IX

Against the prohibition of Rome concerning free access to the Bible by the common people, Diodati affirms the concept of the "perspicuity" of Scripture. He says, "The obscurity in Scripture is not such that the doctrines of faith may not be authenticated clearly and manifestly...."

Diodati does not deny some difficulties in understanding the message of the Scriptures. There is some obscurity in the Bible; indeed, "Thy word doth abound in mysteries," he acknowledges,[213] but not to such an extent as to require the mediation of church and tradition. Francis Turretin insisted:

> The papists, not satisfied with their endeavours to prove the Scriptures insufficient in order to bring in the necessity of tradition, began to question their perspicuity (as if the sense could by no one be ascertained with certainty without the judgement of the church) in order to have a pretext for keeping the people from their perusal. Having concealed the candle under a bushel, they reign in darkness more easily.[214]

Diodati's thesis must be understood in the light of this debate.

Explaining 2 Corinthians 4:3, Diodati says in the *Annotations* that the apostle "shows that the blindness of unbelievers derogates nothing from the perspicuity of that doctrine which he preached." On another passage, he asserts that when Moses said that the commandment is "not hidden" (Deut. 30:11), he intended to say not "so wonderfully above thee that [most do] not comprehend it," because this expression is related "to the clear manifestation of God's will made unto his people."[215] If Scripture is clear and its meaning not hidden, there is no problem.

The danger in reading Scripture, Diodati makes clear, is not from Scripture itself, "but from human recklessness." He argues that the blindness of man should not be confused with the obscurity of Scripture. The terms should not be inverted, making the supposed obscurity of Scriptures the cause of the ignorance or the mistakes of man. It cannot be concluded that the light of the sun is dark simply because someone who is blind asserts that he cannot see it. Natural man, the one "who hath no other light but the natural reason of his soul, wanting the gift of the Holy Ghost,"[216] does not receive the clear truth of God because "man's soul and understanding only can know man's secret thoughts."[217] Natural man possesses only "the carnal understanding and judgment" which "hath no proportion nor concordancy, but only with worldly things, and cannot reach to divine and heavenly ones."[218]

That is why, according to Diodati, David asks God: "Amend in me my natural ignorance; giving me the lively light of thy Spirit; by which I may apprehend thy Law in its spiritual sense, and thy whole word in the Mysteries of thy promised salvation; which are otherwise incomprehensible to the flesh."[219] Left to himself, man is unable to see the clear light of God's truth because "in this world we are vivified, and enlightened in a lively faith, and saving knowledge, by the Spirit of grace."[220] Therefore, "seeing that carnal men have no light nor knowledge of God's secrets, how can they judge of, or censure that which his Spirit doth dictate to believers?"[221]

Hence, while the Church of Rome was engaged in gathering and burning all vernacular Bibles, New Testaments, and other portions of Scripture, as well as every sort of devotional literature, the Reformers and Diodati consecrated their lives "to open the door of the knowledge of celestial truth." With the publication of the *Index Clementinus* in 1596, the fountainhead of faith was stopped up for many people in Europe, especially in Italy where "an individual and direct encounter with the Bible in its integrity would have not been possible any longer to those who did not know Latin," including the great majority of Italians including the clergy.[222] But in that same year, a twenty-years-old Italian refugee in Geneva had already begun his work; Italy would not be left without the light of God's truth.

Comment on Thesis X

After discussing the nature, purpose, identity, canon, and versions of the Scriptures, and the right and duty of all men to read it in their own tongues, Diodati turns to deal with the issue of biblical interpretation. His position on this should be understood in light of the Protestant concept of the perspicuity of the Scriptures. The search for theological clarity led Protestant preachers and scholars to avoid all nebulous exegesis; that is why the Reformation brought about a shift from the allegorical method of exegesis to a more literal interpretation of the Bible. The purpose of this change was to define the fundamental doctrines of the Christian faith plainly enough so that the claims of the Roman Catholic Church concerning the need for the mediation of church and tradition could be shown to be false and misleading. In other words, the issue of the interpretation of the Bible involves a further development of the Protestant principle of *sola Scriptura.*

In his pastoral concern that men should read their Bibles to derive the necessary knowledge for eternal life, Diodati was opposing the Roman Catholic dictum that no one should presume to interpret Scripture "contrary to that sense which holy mother Church—whose it is to judge of the true sense and interpretation of the holy Scriptures—hath held and doth hold, or even contrary to the unanimous consent of the Fathers; even though such interpretations were never [intended] to be at any time published."[223] The problem that Diodati was facing has been well summarized by Francis Turretin: "The papists, in order to force upon us another visible judge of controversies (*viz.*, the church and the pope) besides the Scriptures and the Holy Spirit speaking in them, attribute a manifold sense to them and hence they infer that they are doubtful and ambiguous."[224] Furthermore, beside this polemical purpose, Diodati was concerned with the establishment of a hermeneutic, founded on the principle of *sola Scriptura*, that was able to produce a biblical doctrinal system and, at the same time, to move from exegesis to the application of that system in preaching. For this reason, he affirms that the "meaning of Scripture…is not multiple, but one and uniform."

He builds on the foundation of both the divinity and humanity of the Bible. The Bible is a divine book through which the purpose of the Holy Spirit is made known to men. In the Bible, God reveals Himself to man, and He does so in the language of man so that the meaning of the Scriptures "is understood from the sequence of the words and sentences," according to the one and uniform sense originally and plainly intended by the Holy Spirit. Diodati's assumption is that, because of the uniqueness and simplicity of God, the truth of God is likewise unique and simple. Moreover, the Bible is also a human book, prepared for man and adapted to him. In his first thesis, Diodati had already stated that the Bible is a collection of Scriptures written by "Prophets, Apostles, and Evangelists," and that it is so because it is man who needs to be pointed to God. This assertion implies that man needs to be directed not only primarily, but also plainly and spontaneously, to the mind of God made known in Scripture, which, in turn, presupposes the idea that human language is essentially uniform and has one main sense. For these reasons, according to Diodati, God's message in Scripture has but one uniform sense.

Comment on Thesis XI
In her first work on Diodati, Milka Ventura repeatedly explains that he chooses "a literal exegesis." She says that he is very "cautious and diligent in applying the theory of Scripture *interpres sui*" and, fleeing from

"forced interpretations even when they could confirm some fundamental dogma," he wants "to make clear what the biblical verses really signify."[225] Hence, in order to be consistent in the application of the principle of *sola Scriptura*, Diodati explains further that "allegory, anagogy, and tropology are not varied meanings of Scripture, but varied natural applications, and cannot be used for the establishment of the dogmas of faith."

As suggested in Chapter 2, the so-called "varied meanings" of the Scriptures had been challenged already during the Middle Ages. The opposition of the school of Antioch to allegorical exegesis is well documented. David S. Dockery explains that "the artificiality of much allegorical interpretation...could not fail to cause a negative response, and the outright rejection of allegorical exegesis was centered in Antioch."[226] In Jerome, Augustine, and Theodoret, elements of literal and figurative interpretation are present, but their main concern was to communicate the canonical meaning of Scripture; in other words, they aimed to exegete passages and texts of the Bible by interpreting them in and according to the context of the whole of Scripture.

Later in the Middle Ages, although there was no outright rejection of the varied applications of Scripture, the priority of the literal sense was stressed to the point that its meaning was considered to determine the other senses. Muller shows two directions taken in the development of medieval exegesis: one towards a fourfold exegesis (literal, allegorical, tropological, and anagogical) and the other, though not opposed to the spiritualizing of texts, towards a literal interpretation.[227] It is evident, therefore, that the shift away from the allegorical and towards the literal method is not something that first occurred during the Reformation.

Moreover, Luther, Calvin, and the other Reformers did not merely exchange allegory for literalism. They rather reinforced the move towards the literal method by stressing textual and philological studies and proceeding to find various figures and shades of meaning in allegory (what is to be believed: *credenda*), in tropology (what is to be done: *agenda*), and in anagogy (what is to be hoped: *speranda*). "This passage from the fourfold exegesis toward an exegesis emphasizing the literal meaning of the text, therefore, marks a continuity—not a contrast—between sixteenth-century biblical interpretation and the exegesis of at least the preceding four centuries."[228]

This continuity is clearly expressed in Diodati's thesis. In his formulation, the honesty and humility of both the Reformers and Diodati himself are revealed. In fact, even if opposed to the Roman Catholic claim that no one could interpret the Bible "contrary to that sense which holy mother Church—whose it is to judge of the true sense and interpretation of the holy Scriptures—hath held and doth hold," they did not altogether despise the past nor the teachings of Roman Catholic theologians. What has been said of Calvin is applicable also to Diodati: "His attacks on allegory are not directed against the *sensus allegoricus*, but against an over-elaborated use of allegory…as well as against an allegorical interpretation imposed arbitrarily on a passage."[229] For this reason, Diodati is careful to explain that he is not opposed to allegorical interpretation *per se*, but rather to its abuses, especially those seeking to confirm some dogma apart from or contrary to the witness of Scripture.

The fact that Diodati does not depart from past exegesis and that there is an exegetical continuity between the Reformation and medieval exegesis is made plain in his *Annotations*. Commenting on Hosea 12:10, he says, "*similitudes*] *viz*. Grave sentences and doctrines illustrated with similitudes, according to the Holy Ghost's ordinary style." On Matthew 13:3:

> *In parables*] This was a kind of teaching used amongst the Jews, and followed by our Savior, as very useful to make the truth known, and to cause the apprehension to enter into the spirit of the hearers by a well appropriated similitude of some framed narration: wherein a parable differs from an Allegory, which takes the figure of a true history, but in a various sense to represent moral or spiritual things; and from an enigma which hath more obscurity and brevity than a parable; and from a plain similitude inserted in the natural and proper extent of the discourse, and is therefore clear and plain to be understood.

His notes on 1 Corinthians 10:2 make a similar point:

> *Were all*] The meaning is, As the deliverance out of Egypt was a figure of the redemption by Christ; and the pilgrimage through the wilderness, an image of the elect's life in the world; and the land of Canaan, a shadow of the kingdom of heaven: so the passage through the Red Sea, and the being under the cloud, were a sacred figure correspondent to Baptism: and Manna, and the water coming out of the rock, a sign which had its relation to the Lord's Supper.

Concerning the allegory in Galatians 4, Diodati explains: "*Are an allegory*] viz. Besides the historical and literal sense, they may be taken for a figure of God's great family." It is clear that Diodati does not reject absolutely and definitively allegory, tropology, and anagogy; rather, he asserts their subordination to the literal sense and to the principle of *sola Scriptura* in order to make clear that they could not be used or abused to confirm the dogmas of faith.

In conclusion, Diodati's hermeneutic helps protect interpreters of the Bible from the abuses of the past. However, it also delivers them from the limitations of the modern critical method because it demands "the exegete move past the rather bare grammatical meaning of the text to doctrine, morality and hope—in short, from *littera* to *credenda, agenda,* and *speranda.*"[230]

Comment on Theses XII, XIII, and XIV

With these three theses, Diodati defines even more precisely the proper application of the principle *sola Scriptura*. First of all, he explains that "the judge of every interpretation is the Holy Spirit speaking in the Scriptures."

It has been shown already that Diodati strongly emphasized the right and duty of all men to read the Scriptures. This, however, does not mean that men can rise above the Scriptures in order to judge them. The supremacy of the authority of the Bible is the primary question "and almost the only one on account of which all the other controversies about the Scriptures were started."[231] The necessity of affirming clearly and precisely the authority, integrity, purity, perspicuity, and perfection of Scripture was determined by the attempt of the Roman Catholic Church to prove that the Bible could not be the supreme judge of all interpretation, so that she could show the necessity of the mediation of the church. This is why Diodati states that the testimony of the Spirit of God in the Scriptures is the supreme judge of biblical interpretation.

Accordingly, he says: "the Spirit of God . . . kindleth in us [believers] the knowledge of God, and of the mysteries belonging to our salvation. *That we might know]* namely, by a certain knowledge; for the nature of faith is not to doubt at all, but with full assurance to receive all God's promises." The natural man cannot obtain this knowledge because he has "no other light but the natural reason of his soul, wanting the gift of the Holy Spirit…. *Spiritually]* viz. by a divine light and judgment, according to the principles and rules of God's Spirit." And he adds that "the man that is enlightened and regenerated by God's Spirit...understands and discerns all God's truth...sealed and rooted in his heart by the Holy Ghost, no way depending on human judgment."[232]

Therefore, because of man's inability to know God, the only voice that can speak and impart the truth to him is that of the Spirit as heard in Scripture. The Spirit makes His voice heard to men objectively in the Scriptures, but also subjectively through Scripture. According to the historic trinitarian theology of Christianity, Diodati stresses that the Holy Ghost is the Spirit of truth, hence "the true author of all divine inspiration...which accompanieth the truth of his word to seal and persuade it...by his secret and internal inspirations and persuasions."[233] Christ came to "bear witness unto the truth" (John 18:37), and the Spirit that He poured forth upon His church continues to pour out through the very instrument that Christ used, namely, the written Word of God. For this reason, "the only means to be partaker of...everlasting life is by the operation of the Holy Ghost, who engenders the true faith in men's hearts."[234] It is especially the place "of the Holy Ghost's working in the most holy Trinity...especially in the elect, in whose hearts it is the property of the Holy Spirit of grace to imprint only the doctrine of Christ."[235]

For this reason, Diodati asserts further that private spirits or individuals cannot judge the Bible because "the testimony of the Holy Spirit in the Scriptures is public." The decree of the Council of Trent on the Scriptures had as its aim "to restrain petulant spirits" in order to establish the interpretation of the Bible according to "that sense which holy mother Church hath held and doth hold." For Rome, the "petulant spirits" were the Protestants who gave free access to the Bible for all people. But Diodati—representative of the best Reformed tradition[236]—also speaks about some pretending "private spirits": "We must especially beware of understanding or interpreting them [the prophets] according to every man's mind or understanding, but according to the meaning of the Holy Ghost which revealeth itself, either by the clear events of the Gospel, or by the divine inspirations and expositions of the Apostles, or by the comparing of the same Prophets, and their continual content."[237] According to these words, the true interpretation of the Bible is not to be derived from some external source; Scripture is to be explained from Scripture (*Scripturam ex Scriptura explicandam esse*).

The conclusion of Diodati's reasoning is therefore quite obvious: "We attribute to the Church, Councils, Doctors, and Pastors no authority except the ministerial one of interpreting the Scriptures." The problem here is understanding the meaning of the phrase "except the ministerial one." It seems almost as if this assertion contains a contradiction. In reality, however, Diodati's thesis is a reflection of a triple distinction on the concept of authority. There is, first, a supreme or absolute authority; that is God's authority as expressed in the Scriptures. Secondly, there is a subordinate or ministerial authority through which Scripture is interpreted and applied. Thirdly, there is a private authority that, after having received some truth from the first two authorities, judges on its own. The judgment of the first is final and absolute; the second gives a public judgment that is nevertheless subordinate and in accordance with the determinations of the first authority; and the third gives a judgment of private discretion with no public weight. Therefore, Diodati is affirming that the authority of churches, councils, doctors, and pastors remains always subordinate to the authority of God as it is revealed in Scripture. These authorities are at best secondary or ministerial, in the sense that they serve under the final and supreme authority of the Bible. Although the church and her ministers may judge controversies of faith, they must judge them according to the word of God, and no one can dare to establish another absolute and infallible authority besides the Scriptures.

Comment on Thesis XV
In this thesis, Diodati affirms the principle of *sola Scriptura* in a positive way, declaring that "the most faithful rule of every interpretation is the analogy of faith." The *analogia fidei* is that method of interpretation according to which the general teaching of Scripture on a given subject, understood by the more clear or unambiguous biblical passages, determines the meaning of less clear or ambiguous texts related to the same subject. This means that the work of exegesis and interpretation presupposed for the Protestant preachers and scholars a uniform theological sense of Scripture and took place in a confessional context. In other words, exegesis was not for them an end in itself, but "a path—a *methodus*—leading to theological formulation on all matters of doctrine and of practice."[238] Hence, the exhaustive harmony of sense in the message of the Bible operates as an interpretative frame that is determinative of all interpretations. This underlying coherence shows that the analogy of faith is synonymous with the *analogia Scripturae*, the interpretation of a biblical passage by way of comparison with other passages.

This was the method both advocated and followed by Diodati. For example, commenting on John 6:51, he states:

> *Is my flesh*] that is to say, I am the sacred food of the soul, for as much as in my humanity I will offer my self to death as an expiatory sacrifice for the sins of the world, and that this my flesh is eaten by the soul, that is to say, applied to life by the actual

commemoration, lively faith, and inward apprehension, to be rejoiced, comforted, strengthened, and sustained in the fruition and feeling of God's grace, which is the spiritual life. And it seems that Christ hath made use of these terms by reason that in all ancient religions, true and false, it was a sign of communion to that which one professed, to eat of the flesh of the sacrifices, 1 Cor. 10.18. Heb. 13.10. and all to show that every Christian ought to have part in Christ, to unite him and appropriate him to himself by a lively faith, which worketh with Christ, as eating doth upon flesh; and without which Christ doth man no good, no more than meat which is not eaten nor concocted, doth not nourish the body.

In these devotional and pastoral annotations, Diodati explains that the expression "is my flesh" must be intended as an offering of Christ's "self to death as an expiatory sacrifice for the sins of the world." In his comment, he introduces the idea of atonement for sin, but where did he find it? He had already explained that, when Jesus said, "My Father gives you the true bread from heaven" (John 6:32), He was referring to His abasing Himself and taking human flesh for the world's salvation. He also makes reference to Christ's words in John 3:13: "No one has ascended to heaven but He who came down from heaven, that is, the Son of Man who is in heaven." Moreover he does not fail to notice that in the same context there is an analogous expression that points to a sacrificial meaning of the words of Christ, and he explains that the expiation is "made by the shedding of his blood."[239] Therefore his interpretation is determined in part by an analogy with the teaching of the Gospel of John on the incarnation and on the propitiatory sacrifice of Christ. Furthermore, he points out that Christ chooses these words expressly because of a linguistic habit of all ancient religions, according to which the eating of the sacrifices is a "sign of communion" with the deity, justifying his assertion by quoting two passages outside John's Gospel. It is quite clear that Diodati is interpreting John 6:51 not only in the light of the general tenor of the Gospel of John, but also within the broader context of Scripture.

Another instance may be found in Romans 1:4:

> *Declared*] As by a solemn and sovereign sentence, Psal. 2.7 to be the true Son of God, against all the false judgments, calumnies, contradictions and doubts of the world, Luke 1.35, I Tim. 3.16. See Acts 13.33. *According to*] namely, according to his divine nature (called Spirit, I Tim. 3.16, Heb. 9.14, I Pet. 3.18) which was before covered under the infirmity of the flesh; but in his resurrection and after it hath been manifested and showed in divine power and glory, by effects which were altogether to be admired.

This is again an example that demonstrates how Scripture in general, together with a comparison of specific texts, functioned as a theological framework valid for biblical exegesis and interpretation.

In her analysis of Diodati's *Annotations*, Milka Ventura states that "it is characteristic of his comment not to look for explanations and confirmations outside Scripture itself."[240] In both her works, Ventura emphasizes that Diodati translates as a theologian. Her purpose is to show that he considered knowledge of the original languages only as a necessary instrument for understanding the text, and that to him the most important thing was the content. She affirms that "Diodati reveals himself to be more of an interpreter than a translator of Scripture,"[241] adding that his personality was "dogmatic and intolerant" and that he was very rigid in his defense of an "immutable and canonized truth that he considered conquered once and for all."[242] As in the case of many others, her assessment of Diodati is heavily influenced by the work of Bergeaud on the history of the University of Geneva. Bergeaud maintains that, at the beginning of the seventeenth century, the Genevan Academy suffered a radical transformation because the humanistic element of the teaching lost its scientific autonomy, becoming subordinate to theology.[243] F. W. Farrar expresses a very similar opinion in his influential *History of Interpretation*. He argues that orthodoxy read the Bible "by the unnatural glare of theological hatred" and "imposed the senses of men upon the words of God," making the analogy of faith and the analogy of Scripture "the pretext for regarding the Bible as a sort of quartz-bed, in which was to be found the occasional gold of a proof text."[244] The extreme attitudes of some exponents of Protestant orthodoxy may properly be condemned, but Diodati was thoroughly convinced that, where different translations were possible, the biblical witness and its theological frameworks must determine the right one.[245]

Comment on Thesis XVI

Thus far, Diodati has not dealt with the Scriptures in their direct relationship with the church as an institution. He mentioned the church in Thesis XIV, but only to discuss the problem of the interpretation of the Bible. All his straightforward propositions regarding the Scriptures imply a certain view concerning the relationship between the Scriptures and the church, and between their respective authorities; hence all of them must be read against the background of the controversy with the Church of Rome. Yet, up to this point Diodati has not discussed this issue directly. However, from Thesis XVI onwards, he concentrates especially on this theme.

Diodati begins his attempt to define the nature of the relationship between Scripture and church by saying, "Scripture is trustworthy by and in virtue of itself, and does not need the precarious authority of the Church." This is another clear affirmation of the idea that in all matters of faith and practice the supreme authority is *sola Scriptura*. All that Diodati has been discussing concerning Scripture is determined by his aim of holding to this principle. At the time of the Reformation, the goal of the Roman Catholic Church was to establish some criterion by virtue of which the authority of the church could remain above that of Scripture. It is for this reason that Diodati addresses the subject of the identity of the authority that makes known the supreme authority of the Scriptures.

In his annotation upon 1 Timothy 3:15 he comments, "*The pillar*] *viz*. By whose Ministry the authority, dignity, knowledge, virtue, and use of the truth of the Gospel ought to be preserved in the world, and maintained against all errors, contradictions and corruptions." Here he identifies two functions of the church: the preservation and the defense of the truth of Scripture. If the duty of the church were to confer authority or to authenticate Scripture, Diodati would have surely recognized that in this context. Moreover, commenting on Matthew 16:8, he explains that Christ assures Peter that the doctrine that he would have been preaching would have been the foundation of the church, "worthy to be absolutely believed *without any further proof*, as immediately inspired by God" (emphasis added). It is evident that, for Diodati, the authority of the Bible is not founded upon the church, for the simple reason that the church itself is founded upon the authority of the Bible. It is the doctrine communicated infallibly by the apostles through the Holy Spirit that constitutes the foundation of the church, as he emphasizes on the basis of passages such as Ephesians 2:20. This apostolic truth does not need "any further proof," because by its own virtue[246] it is a trustworthy guide in all things pertaining to the faith; therefore, the Scriptures themselves are the sole dogmatic authority for the church. This is the reason why Paul and the other apostles taught "the first, most certain, undoubted and fundamental truth of the Gospel, *upon which ought to be founded, and by which ought to be ruled,* all the doctrine of those who come after."[247]

These quotations show that Diodati's discussion thus far concerning the origin, the necessity, the purity, and the perspicuity of Scripture is significant because of this very question of authority. Those attributes of the Scriptures are sufficient to make them fully trustworthy; and because they are trustworthy, they are also authoritative.

It is also worthy of note that, for Diodati, the perfect trustworthiness of the Bible is a reflection of the perfect trustworthiness of God Himself. If the Bible is not trustworthy in itself, God is not trustworthy in Himself; the Bible is His Word, and a word *of God* cannot but reflect the essential attributes without which God could not be God. Commenting on Psalm 138:2, Diodati paraphrases: "Over and above the glory and the praise, which is due unto thee for thy other perfections, thou art also more extolled in the effects of the truth of thy promise towards me: Or, *thou hast magnified thy name above all things through thy word*; namely, it being considered either in its infallible truth, or in its most powerful virtue and operation" (emphasis added). Although Diodati is not speaking here directly about the nature and the attributes of Scriptures as being a reflection of God's nature and attributes, it is clearly his opinion that the manifestation of the glories of God's name is something achieved also "through the word being considered in its infallible truth" and "in its most powerful virtue and operation."

Comment on Theses XVII, XVIII, and XIX
It has already been noted in this chapter that Diodati is careful to explain that the Spirit makes His voice heard to men objectively in the Scriptures, but also subjectively through Scripture.[248] Now he relates the reality of the doctrine of the Spirit to the issue of the trustworthiness (and therefore authority) of the Bible and affirms: "By and in virtue of itself it is also believed by believers, because the teaching authority and anointing of the Spirit work inwardly." In this way, Diodati develops positively his claim that the authority of the church, when confronted with that of Scripture, is "precarious" or uncertain. It should be remembered that Diodati grew up with a very clear understanding of the precarious authority of the church. The Reformers, and Calvin in particular, also had a clear understanding of this when challenged by the Roman Catholic theologians with Augustine's well-known declaration that he would not have believed the Gospel apart from the authority of the Roman Catholic Church.[249] Accordingly, in these three theses, Diodati explains why and how the Scriptures are the only source of authority and what is the true function of the church.

Following the example of the great Reformers, Diodati manifests a great respect for the church. He does not consider it mechanically as an ordered and structured body acting through the leadership of an official hierarchy, but as the communion of saints (*communio sanctorum*) and the body of Christ (*corpus Christi*). However, he does not fall into the mistake of regarding the authority of this body as superior to that of Scripture, and he regards that authority as something not original but only derived from Scripture. His purpose is not to abolish the role of the church nor its derivative authority, but to correct those aberrations developed in the course of many centuries that brought about a subordination of Scripture to the authority of the church. To do that he explains, first of all, the concept of the *testimonium Spiritus sancti* that was formulated by Calvin and became the foundation of the Protestant doctrine of authority. According to the classical statement of this doctrine, the Holy Spirit of God, the third person of the Trinity, works inwardly in men to testify concerning the truth of Scripture. Therefore there are two *principia cognoscendi*: one is external, namely, the written Word; the other is internal (cognitive foundations), namely, the faith of the heart which, resting on the testimony of the Spirit, is enabled to recognize and respond to God's calling through the external Word.

As Theses XII, XIII, and XIV have indicated, Diodati upholds the same principle. Paraphrasing John 14:26, he states in the *Annotations*: "It is true that I teach you by my *outward word*, which as yet you do not very well apprehend, but the Spirit shall give you a lively and *internal understanding* of it" (emphasis added). Speaking about the preaching of the apostle Paul, he says: "*Demonstration*] That is to say, hath been animated by the divine efficacy of the Holy Ghost, with which God doth accompany his word rightly preached, to enlighten the minds and persuade the hearts.... *In the power*] Namely, grounded upon, and subsisting in that powerful and invincible internal persuasion of God's Spirit."[250] The Spirit therefore "beareth witness" in two ways, "outwardly by the word, and inwardly in the heart of every believer."[251]

But if the efficient cause by which people are induced to believe in the divine truth of Scripture is the Holy Spirit, what of the church? Far from neglecting it, Diodati is careful to make clear that the church is a means through which people believe: "The Holy Spirit uses certain means, through which He communicates Himself into the minds of men: among these [means], the decision and witness of the Church have a place." Diodati's student, Francis Turretin, elaborates as follows: "If the question is why, or on account of what do I believe the Bible to be divine, I will answer that I do so on account of the Scripture itself which by its marks proves itself to be such. If it is asked whence or from what I believe, I will answer from the Holy Spirit who produces that belief in me. Finally, if I am asked by what means or instrument I believe it, I will answer through the church which God uses in delivering the Scriptures to me."[252] Therefore Diodati—in company with all the so-called epigones—does not question the fact that the Spirit uses means in inwardly persuading men of the authority of Scripture, and that among these means the church has a prominent place.

The position of the church in relationship to Scripture is not a minor issue because, in some sense, the church itself confirms the authority of Scripture. Diodati is affirming that the church has a role of evaluation and witness in that the testimony of the whole church from the beginning is to be considered as an evidence of the divinity of the Scriptures.[253] Turretin includes the witness of the *communio sanctorum* among the external marks through which the Bible proves its own divine authority:

> Finally, the consent of all people who, although differing in customs (also in opinion about sacred things, worship, language and interest), have nevertheless received this word as a valuable treasury of divine truth and have regarded it as the foundation of religion and the worship of God. It is impossible to believe that God would have suffered

so great a multitude of men, earnestly seeking him, to be so long deceived by lying books.[254]

The obvious conclusion reached by Diodati is that "[a teaching] can be believed through the Church, [but] to believe because of the Church is not faith." In subsequent theses, he will explain the reason why this is so.

Comment on Theses XX and XXI

The first reason why true faith cannot depend on the church but must be founded on Scripture alone is that only Scripture "contains most completely all things necessary to salvation."

At the beginning of his theses, Diodati affirmed that, because the Scriptures are of divine origin, it is possible to derive from them "all knowledge necessary for eternal life." At this point in the development of his reasoning, he is going back to the subject of the sufficiency of Scripture not only generally, but in order to address directly the very controversial problem of the so-called "oral or unwritten traditions."

Speaking of the blessed man of Psalm 1, who has his delight in the law of the Lord, he says that God's revealed Word is "the ground of his faith" and that he draws the comfort of his conscience "out of the Promises of grace" and the rule of his life "out of his commandments." He concludes by asserting, "And out of his doctrine, the light of his instruction to salvation."[255] According to Diodati, the Gospel is the power of God unto salvation in the sense that it is "the only most effectual means to save man, by faith in Christ, who is proposed in the Gospel, whereas man in his own nature was not sufficient thereunto." He then continues in his comment on this passage by saying: "He [the apostle Paul] proves that by the Gospel man obtains life and salvation: namely, because it presents unto him the only cause of life, namely, the true righteousness which is

Christ's imputed to man through grace, and embraced by him by a lively faith."[256] This evangelical exclusivity is for Diodati a direct reflection of the teaching of Christ. In fact, commenting on John 14:6 he paraphrases: "*I am*] In me is the means to get that life, and that glory which I myself go unto, I do give the most assured declaration and direction by my word, and by my Spirit I do confer that life upon men." Christ, as he is set forth in the Gospel, is "that meat which endureth unto everlasting life," namely, the doctrine of the Gospel and Christ Himself "who is proposed in it." This spiritual food "is not bodily food that perisheth itself and cannot keep the body from perishing: but the food of the soul which liveth and causeth to live eternally."[257] For Diodati, therefore, Scripture is sufficient for the salvation of men because it is a word "which liveth," a word "which is endowed with an effectual and spiritual power, and is established and lasteth for ever, whereby it is likewise capable to bring forth the spiritual and everlasting life in believers."[258]

Having shown that everything necessary to salvation is contained in Scripture, Diodati proceeds to clarify that "Scripture is therefore necessary." As already seen, this necessity has been determined by the sinful condition of man, and by his inability to find and turn to God in his own power. Because of his natural blindness, man is in need of a special revelation coming directly from God in order to understand the chief end of the life of the universe and the truth that can lead him to his God and to happiness. Therefore, intending the word *Scripture* in the material sense attributed to it by the Genevan school,[259] Diodati affirms that "those things cannot be sought elsewhere." The doctrine necessary to salvation is a revelation that comes from God alone; it is contained only in Scripture, and it is therefore impossible to come to this saving teaching from a different source or in a different manner. These things are explained by Richard Muller in the following way:

> As a final argument of their theological prolegomena, many of the Reformed orthodox argued that theology has two *principia* or foundations, the essential foundation (*principium essendi*) and the cognitive foundation (*principium cognoscendi*)—God and Scripture. These two foundations are both necessary. Without God, there can be no word concerning God, no theology; without the scriptural revelation, there can be no genuine or authoritative word concerning God, and, again, no theology.[260]

According to Diodati, the Hebrews were accustomed to use the expression "word of God" to indicate "God himself manifesting himself,"[261] and when God spoke to men "by his Son," He declared fully "his whole counsel concerning the salvation of mankind."[262] This is the reason why the faith of those who have believed has for its foundation not the church and its unwritten traditions, but "the doctrine of the old and new Testament, the principal subject whereof is Christ."[263] Diodati therefore comments on John 1:18 as follows: "No man of himself hath access, nor communication of knowledge, nor grace with God, but only by the means of his Son; who in his person is the lively and perfect portraiture of the Father, *John 14.9. 2 Cor.4.4. Col. 1.15. Heb 1.3* and by his doctrine represents him to salvation." On Ephesians 3:3 he relates God's revelation to its embodiment in Scripture: "*By revelation*] He means that which was revealed unto him when he was appointed to be an apostle.... *The mystery*] namely, the sacred doctrine of the Gospel incomprehensible to human understanding."

These remarks make very clear how the Genevan school represented by Diodati explained the interdependency of the necessity of revelation and the necessity of Scripture for man's salvation. For Calvin, Beza, Diodati, and Turretin, there is no other way through which men can know and obtain salvation apart from the revelation of God's saving word; and since a saving word from God is necessary, Scripture is necessary, because it is not possible to come to this saving word in any other way.

Comment on Theses XXII, XXIII, and XXIV

These theses again represent a reaction to the decree of the Council of Trent on the Scriptures. The teaching of the Reformers is reflected in Diodati's statement, according to which "To say that the Scriptures are only for the well being of the Church (as they say) is ungodly." It seems that the young Diodati is denying once more (as he did earlier in Thesis XIV) the presumption of the exclusive right of interpretation of Scripture by the Roman Church. He is in fact careful to explain in his *Annotations* that the Scriptures are for the benefit of all. Commenting on Isaiah 8:20, he affirms: "*To the law*] That is to say, turn to God alone, who by his law declares his will unto you: which you must observe, and *by his Prophets he witnesseth his good toward you*, whereupon you must hope" (emphasis added). He was of the opinion that the good and happiness of man in general have their source in the Scriptures, and he explains that it is Christ who "makes us *happy*, when he unites us unto him *by his Word*."[264] In fact, while considering Christ's declaration, "Blessed are they that have not seen, and yet have believed" (John 20:29), he assures his readers that the ground of this blessedness is "the bare word of God."

This relationship between the idea of the good of man in general and the knowledge of God through Scripture is very plainly a reflection of one of the basic features of the Reformed understanding of true religion. As Calvin had taught the Genevan church, man's chief good and joy are found only in the true knowledge of God. In 1545, Calvin published a catechism to instruct the churches of Geneva that came to be known affectionately as "Calvin's Catechism" for more than three centuries throughout the Reformed world. As a boy at Geneva College and then as a theological student at the Academy, Diodati repeated and consider many times the following questions and answers:

Master. What is the chief end of human life?

Scholar. To know God by whom men were created.

M. What reason have you for saying so?

S. Because he created us and placed us in this world to be glorified in us. And it is indeed right that our life, of which himself is the beginning, should be devoted to his glory.

M. What is the highest good of man?

S. The very same thing.

M. Why do you hold that to be the highest good?

S. Because without it our condition is worse than that of the brutes.

M. Hence, then, we clearly see that nothing worse can happen to a man than not to live to God.

S. It is so.[265]

Diodati was thus nurtured from his earliest days in the understanding that the Bible is the foundation of man's good and blessedness, and this for him meant that to say that Scripture was a private possession of the ecclesiastical hierarchy was ungodly.

The Council of Trent (as seen earlier in Chapter 2) had declared that the truth of the Gospel is the fountain of both saving truth and moral discipline, and that "this truth and discipline are contained in the written books, and the unwritten traditions which, received from the Apostles from the mouth of Christ himself, or from the Apostles themselves, the Holy Ghost dictating, have come down even unto us, transmitted as it were from hand to hand." So strong was the persuasion of the Roman Church that the same canon declared: "If any one receive not, as sacred and canonical, the said books entire with all their parts, as they have been used to be read in the Roman Church, and as they are contained in the old Latin vulgate edition; and knowingly and deliberately contemn the traditions aforesaid; *let him be anathema.*"[266] These declarations make plain the problem facing the Reformers and Diodati and why, on the one hand, they advocated that Scripture is the source of truth and foundation of good for man in general, while, on the other hand, they rejected the so-called unwritten traditions.

Thus, after having stated positively that "Scripture contains most completely all things necessary for salvation," Diodati adds negatively that "unwritten traditions are not necessary for salvation." It is clear that he is concerned only about the weight placed upon traditions with regard to the salvation of man from sin and judgment. The state of the question is succinctly put by Turretin: "The question then amounts to this—whether the Scripture perfectly contains all things (not absolutely), but necessary to salvation; not expressly and in so many words, but equivalently and by legitimate inference, as to leave no place for any unwritten (*agraphon*) word containing doctrinal or moral traditions. Is the Scripture a complete and adequate rule of faith and practice or only a partial and inadequate rule? We maintain the former."[267]

In his *Annotations*, Diodati gives a Protestant definition of the nature of these traditions: "*The tradition*] This word, with the addition *your*, or *of men*, or *of the Elders*, or the like, signifieth a doctrine, order, or observance touching God's service instituted by men, and kept from father to son, not out of God's express word."[268] These traditions are not necessarily or intrinsically evil; indeed, they might have a legitimate function with regard to the policy of the church. Commenting on the traditions of the Jews, Diodati says that "some were laudable, concerning the order and decency of the Jewish Church, in things indifferent."[269] Yet, "others were superstitious; and others wicked and abominable," so that those who uphold them make of none effect the truth of God: "*Of non effect*] *viz.* ye are the cause that the commandment is broken by your doctrine, which teacheth men's consciences to have more respect to these vicious oaths than to Gods express law; and all by reason of the superstitious esteem, in which you hold these ceremonies above true and real piety."[270]

Diodati thought that there were occasions within the churches for unwritten rules, for these "concern only church polity" in a positive and constructive way. Commenting on the ordinances delivered by Paul to the Corinthians, he says: "*In all things*] Namely, all my doctrines, instructions, and rules concerning manners, and the public order of the Church.... *The ordinances*] he means especially the rules concerning the order and government of the Church."[271] He is of the opinion that these ordinances or rules might be divided into two categories: those things taught by the Scriptures that bind the conscience, and those occasional, mutable, and local practices that do not bind the conscience of all Christians in every place and epoch. Thus, speaking about the delivery of those decrees ordained of the apostles and elders at Jerusalem that had to be kept, he explains, "*The decrees*] He means the decrees which the Apostles had ordained according to the word of God, for they would not bind the consciences in such things as are not contained therein."[272] He regards an apostolic ordinance to abstain from certain kinds of food in the following way: "This is an Ecclesiastical ordinance, and as they call it Canonical; not so much to rule the conscience, and the inward man, as the external action, for the peace, comeliness, and order of the Church *of those days*, in things which of their own nature were indifferent as the eating of blood, or strangled meat."[273] For the Genevan school of theology, therefore, there was a legitimate place for unwritten ordinances or traditions with reference to minor issues in the conduct of the churches.

Nevertheless, as far as pontifical traditions were concerned, the Reformers were united in their views that there was no link to the teaching of Christ and his Apostles. In the Gospel of Matthew, Christ gave to the apostles the mandate to make disciples from every nation, teaching them to observe all things that he had commanded (28:18-20). Diodati explains this saying of Jesus in the following way: "*I have commanded*] Not giving them way to make new commandments: for he will himself possess the power and sovereignty over his Church." Christ admittedly taught many things to His disciples that were not written (cf. John 20:30; 21:25); yet the rules, the ordinances, and the principles that are normative for the life of the Christian churches, whether they belong to doctrine or practice, are contained in the Scriptures. The mandate entrusted by Christ to His church has as its focal point the stewardship of the gospel, as Diodati indicates in his comment on an important passage for the controversy with Rome:

I will give unto thee] That is, I will make thee the steward of my Gospel, and of the spiritual goods of my house; an office signified by carrying the keys, *Isa. 22.22. Revel. 3.7.* so is the doctrine of faith called the key of the kingdom of heaven, *Luke 11.52.* and the Ministers of the Gospel the Stewards, *Luke 12.42. I Cor. 4.1. Titus 1.7. I Peter 4.10. Bind*] a similitude taken from Overseers of great houses, who had authority over the slaves, to punish them with imprisonment, irons, or any other way, to show the authority of the Ministry of the word, *Mat. 18.17. John 20.23.* over the members of the Church, for to exercise a reasonable discipline over them, to tie and captivate their consciences by censures and denunciations of God's judgments, and exclude them from the external communion of the Church by excommunication for their errors: or contrariwise to restore and absolve them upon their conversion and repentance: *and all this ministerially and declaratively, not by a full power, and absolutely, but by virtue of the commission which they have from God, and the rule which is prescribed unto them; beside which all action of the Minister is void before God, and can neither bind nor free the conscience.*[274]

In this way, the young Diodati rejected those declarations of the Council of Trent on the Scriptures which, according to historian Hubert Jedin, were meant to be the "foundation of all further dogmatic definitions."[275]

Comment on Thesis XXV

As he reaches the end of his discussion on the doctrine of Scripture, Diodati wants to make plain that his intent is polemic and that his target is the "Pontiffs," "Libertines," and "Enthusiasts." In common with the other Reformers, he establishes the principle that the God of the Bible is recognized in the fullness of His attributes and power, and that His word, revealed through Scripture, is to be acknowledged as our supreme authority. According to this rule, "the spirits" are to be subjected to the examination of the Scriptures rather than allowing a way for them to subject the Scriptures to some form of human judgment.

It seems that the question that troubled people during Diodati's lifetime was the same that troubled mankind from the very beginning: "Hath God said…?" (Gen. 3:1). Speaking of his own days and of the fight for the right understanding of the inspiration and authority of the Bible, Benjamin Warfield of Princeton observed: "The real question, in a word, is not a new question but the perennial old question, whether the basis of our doctrine is to be what the Bible teaches, or what men teach."[276] For Diodati there was no doubt: the basis of doctrine is what the Bible teaches, because the Bible is divine truth, *the* truth.

The concluding declaration of Diodati's theses is indicative of the character of the man, in accordance with the ways he learned from his tutors at the Academy. The attitude of the Genevan school of theology, as represented by Diodati, was marked by a humble submission to the authority of the Bible, linked to a sincere faith in God and a complete lack of trust in man. The way of submission to Scripture was the safest way. It is for this reason that he prayed: "Let me receive thy word by faith, which word is divine and worthy to be both believed and obeyed…. Let me understand and apprehend it, that I may comfort myself in the promises thereof, and may duly fulfill the commandments of it, and let my faith be nourished and increased through understanding and knowledge."[277]

CONCLUSION

In Christo crucifixo est vera theologia et cognitio ("the true doctrine and knowledge of God is in Christ crucified") was the great message of Martin Luther, the fruit of his own struggle for peace with God. In the fullness of time, this message revealed to much of Europe the inconsistency of the sacramental and penitential system of Roman Catholicism, establishing the principle that "the just shall live by faith." The message of Luther and Calvin spread very quickly throughout the states of the Italian peninsula via Venice, the gateway of the Reformation in Italy. The progress of the doctrines of the Reformation through the efforts of various religious communities such as the Augustinians and the Franciscans, of humanist scholars, and of the pious nobility, was such that the Italian Reformation movement, having realized the impossibility of reforming the church from within, hoped to establish a fellowship of Christian communities as an alternative to the Roman system. But while in other European countries this hope became a reality with the help of the nobility in authority, in Italy "no-one dared to undertake such a step because all were thinking of the instantaneous reaction of the Pope with all the weight of his spiritual and temporal authority, authority structured in a tight weft of the financial interests of great noble families, of bankers, and of merchants of the peninsula."[278]

Against this backdrop, John Diodati is a symbol of the significance and consequences of the Reformation in Italy. Having refused to embrace the reform that many of her own children were requesting, the Church of Rome began the terrible repression of the "Lutheran pestilence" in the 1550s. This violent and bloody counter-reformation accomplished two things: it crushed the weak and strengthened those already strong. At this juncture, Diodati's family fled to Geneva from Lucca. Diodati was among the many who continued the Reformation in Italy from outside of Italy. In this respect, it is relevant to remember his evangelistic attempts through the gateway of Venice, even though they were doomed to failure. Yet, in the wake of this failure, he turned his energies in another direction, namely preaching, teaching, and Bible translation. His work not only served the general cause of Reformation in Europe but also constituted one of the most important witnesses to the light of the gospel for Italians of his generation as well as of those that followed. Against this background, Diodati fulfilled a very important role in the history of Protestantism in Italy.

This role was of particular significance because of the importance of the doctrine of Scripture. The debate concerning the Bible and its authority touched the very heart of the controversy between Romanism and Protestantism. Gigliola Fragnito's statement that the real issue was a fight to control the consciences of the people is correct: "It is in this fight to control the consciences that the translation of the Bible takes up a key importance."[279] If the Protestant principle of *sola Scriptura* had been widely accepted in Italy, Roman Catholicism would have received a severe, if not fatal, blow. At the risk of appearing simplistic or restrictive in judgment, it might be suggested that many of the events that determined the history of Europe and beyond resulted from the position taken on this very issue.

There are a number of conclusions that may be drawn from this study of Diodati. First, there was a significant continuity between Diodati's concept of the doctrine of Scripture and that of his predecessors. This observation is particularly important in the light of the debate in recent decades concerning the extent of continuity between the early Reformers and their successors. Richard A. Muller's outstanding four-volume *magnus opus* on the history of post-Reformation dogmatics demonstrates that in all theological *loci* there is an uninterrupted relationship between the work of the early Reformers and that of their successors. Certain doctrines or aspects of doctrines may indeed have been developed to different degrees by different theologians at different times, but the substance of the theological system of the heirs of the Reformers was the same as that of their fathers in the faith. In the case of Diodati, this connection is particularly evident. Not only his theological education, but also his whole upbringing was a reflection of the vision that shaped the life of Geneva and European Protestantism in general. There are virtually no differences among Calvin, Beza, Diodati, and Turretin on the doctrine of Scripture. Moreover, the contents of the theses on such topics as *De Ecclesia, De Purgatorio, De Verbo Dei, De Christo Mediatore,* etc., presented by Diodati's students to obtain their degree, reflect precisely the same theological outlook that characterized the Reformers of the first generations.[280]

Secondly, Diodati's understanding of the doctrine of Scripture was the very foundation of Protestantism. The real issue at stake concerning Scripture at the time of the Reformation was not so much its nature or its inspiration, but its authority, particularly in the light of the whole ecclesiological structure of the Church of Rome. The Roman Catholic claim concerning the absolute authority of the church is based on the idea that the church is an extension of the incarnation of the Son of God: Christ and the church are *"una persona mystica."*[281]

Because of that belief, one of the main objectives of Rome is catholicity. This means that multiplicity must be brought into unity under the authority of the church's hierarchy, which is the expression, promoter, and guarantor of true unity. An essential part of the struggle of the Reformation (as expressed by Diodati in Thesis XIV) was to oppose this teaching by establishing the supreme authority of the Bible above that of "Church, Councils, Doctors, and Pastors."

Thirdly, Diodati's role as a translator of the Bible is of particular significance. His opinions on this matter, found in scattered letters and documents, are gathered together in the long letter written in 1637 to the synod of Alençon. His work is innovative because he adopts the method called *transferre ad sententiam* ("translation according to sense"), namely, "a faithful oratorical translation."[282] In practice, this means that he sought to use language that was "simple, natural, precise, easy to follow, grave, edifying,"[283] respecting the natural patterns of the vernacular language. In his analysis of Diodati's language and style, Sergio Bozzola notices that he writes "linearly and spontaneously," with a tendency to "resolve the phrase in a structure more in conformity to the syntax of the receiving language."[284] He then adds the following assessment: "The syntax of the *Diodatina*[285] seems to be constantly oriented to smooth over wrinkles and to avoid structures that in some ways could prejudice the clarity and simplicity of the construction."[286] In this respect, Diodati follows the important principle of perspicuity, which is a reflection of the nature of the Scriptures themselves. Thus his letter of 1637 to the Synod of Alençon states that Scripture "is not only for the learned, but for the simple and the common man since it is clear and intelligible." The result is that his work is characterized by "transparency and the easy comprehensibility of the translation."[287]

Finally, Diodati's concept of Scripture and its influence on his work as Bible translator deserve attention. For Diodati, the redemptive theology of the Bible confers on it an organic unity that is independent of its readers. Therefore, the awareness of this theological unity served to preserve him from imposing his own ideas on the biblical field of possible meanings. His concept of Scripture is such that he translates "according to the Protestant tradition, but respecting the letter of the original."[288] As a result, "to affirm that Diodati translates as a theologian does not mean that his theological attitude is dogmatic."[289]

Diodati was an important figure in seventeenth-century Europe. He inherited the legacy of Calvin and Beza and represented this tradition in a worthy manner, as many in Italy, Switzerland, France, Holland, and England bore witness. He was not without faults and weaknesses, yet the motives of his heart and the aims of his work were noble and disinterested. The saddest controversy of his life—the publication of his French translation of the Bible—revealed his complete dedication to his self-appointed task and "the deep piety which led him to undertake his work."[290] This dedication and piety characterized all Diodati's pursuits: his missionary activities; his preaching and pastoral ministry; his professorship at the Academy; his involvement in ecclesiastical policy, as at the Synod of Dort; his participation in the civil life of Geneva; and his work as Bible translator. But in addition to his significance in the broader history of Protestantism in Europe, his influence has also been felt among Italians within and outside Italy, both during his life and long afterwards. Speaking of William Tyndale, David Daniell affirmed: "William Tyndale gave us our English Bible...England's greatest contribution to the world for nearly five hundred years."[291] Italians may equally say, "John Diodati gave us our Italian Bible." According to Giorgio Spini, Diodati's "famous Bible translation, for the reason that it remained unsurpassed until the end of the nineteenth century, is the most significant link between the Italian Protestantism of the Reformation and that of the Risorgimento."[292] Diodati and his Italian Bible remain among the principal symbols of Italian Protestantism. Indeed, it might well be argued that his Bible is *the* symbol of Italian Protestantism.

The significance of Diodati's life and work is well summarized in the language of the epistle to the reader written to present to the English public the third edition of his *Pious Annotations* in 1651. Observing that the real confirmation of the usefulness of the Annotations is the esteem and approval shown to Diodati's work by such "reverend divines" as Gouge, Gattaker, Downham, Ley, Reading, Taylor, Pemberton, and Featly, the writer commends Diodati as "a reverend Protestant Divine of the Church of *Geneva*, the most reformed in all *France* [i.e., French-speaking Europe], and famous for the great lights of it, *John Calvin, Theodorus Beza,* and this renowned *John Diodati*, their successor both in place and eminent erudition."

NOTES

Introduction
[1] W. A. McComish, *The Epigones: a Study of the Theology of the Genevan Academy at the Time of the Synod of Dort, with Special Reference to Giovanni Diodati* (Allison Park: Pennsylvania, Pickwick Publications, 1989), p. 188.
[2] Ibid., p. vii.
[3] This is an abridged version by Maria Betts of *Vie de Jean Diodati, Theologien Genevois*, written by E. de Budé (Lousanne, 1869), and published in London in 1905. This biography has also been translated into Italian (Florence, 1870).
[4] W. A. McComish, *The Epigones*, p. 189.
[5] Another biography in Dutch is by G. D. J. Schotel, *Jean Diodati*.
[6] C. Dardier, "Jean Diodati a Nimes 1614," *Bulletin de la Société de l'Histoire du Protestanisme Francais*, 1853.
[7] E. Sauty, "Calvin and Diodati, essay de comparison portant sur la prédestination" (unpublished thesis, Genève, 1940).
[8] J. P. Gabarel, *Histoire de l'Eglise de Genève* (Genève, 1858-1862).
[9] T. Claparède, *Les Pasteurs Génevois d'Origine Lucquoise* (Genève, 1879).
[10] J. B. G. Galiffe, *Le Refugée Italien de Genève aux XVIe et XVIIe siècles* (Genève, 1881).
[11] J. Weill, "Nicolas Antoine, un Pasteur Protestant Brulé a Genève en 1632 pour Crime de Judaisme," *Revue des Ètudes Juives*, 1898.
[12] C. Borgeaud, *Histoire de l'Université de Genève*, volume 1 (Genève: Georg, 1900).
[13] H. Henry, *L'Eglise de Genève* (Genève, 1909).
[14] B. Lescaze, 'Un Itinéraire Spirituelle au XVIIe Siècle : Nicolas Antoine 1602?-1632' (unpublished thesis, Genève, 1969).
[15] An English title would be "The Exegesis of Genesis and the Theology of the Reformation: a Confrontation between Two Commentaries, Brucioli and Diodati" (University of Florence, 1984-85).
[16] Antonio Brucioli was born in Florence at the end of fifteenth century. He translated the entire Bible into Italian and published it in Venice in 1532. Between 1542 and 1546, he published a seven-volume *Comentario su Tutti i Libri dell'Antico e del Nuovo Testamento* (Commentary on all the books of the Old and New Testament) in Venice. He was persecuted for his evangelical faith and his writings. Ventura examines his Commentary on Genesis .
[17] An English title would be "John Diodati and the Translations of the Bible in his Times: the Old Testament" (University of Turin, 1993).

18 The first Italian version of 1607, the second of 1641, the French version of 1644.
19 *La Sacra Bibbia, Tradotta in Lingua Italiana e Commentata da Giovanni Diodati*, M. Ranchetti e M. Ventura eds. (The Holy Bible, translated into Italian and commented by John Diodati, Milano: Mondadori, 1999).
20 For more general bibliographical information about the reformation in Italy, see *Cinquant'anni di Storiografia Italiana sulla Riforma e i Movimenti Ereticali in Italia, 1950-2000*, S. Peyronel ed. (Torino: Claudiana, 2002).
21 A. Milli, *Giovanni Diodati il Traduttore della Bibbia e la Società degli Esuli Protestanti Italiani a Ginevra 1560-1660* (Lausanne: 1908).
22 G. Luzzi, *La Bibbia in Italia. L'Eco della Riforma nella Repubblica Lucchese: Giovanni Diodati e la sua Traduzione Italiana della Bibbia* (Firenze: 1942).
23 R. Coisson, "Giovanni Diodati e la sua Attività Ecclesiastica" (unpublished thesis, Rome: Facoltà Valdese di teologia, 1964).

Chapter 1

24 A. Pascal, *Da Lucca a Ginevra. Studi sull'Emigrazione Religiosa Lucchese nel sec. XVI* (Torino: Paravia 1932), Chapter 1.3. S. Caponetto, *La Riforma Protestante nell'Italia del Cinquecento* (Torino: Claudiana, 1992), Chapter 16.3.
25 M. Fulvio, *Una Famiglia Lucchese: i Diodati* (Lucca: Actum Luce, Rivista di Studi Lucchesi, 1983), p. 16.
26 E. de Budé, *Vie de Jean Diodati, Theologien Genevois* (Lousanne: Georges Bridel Editeur, 1869), p. 17. M. Luzzati, *La Prima Generazione dei Burlamacchi a Ginevra* (Lucca: Actum Luce, Rivista di Studi Lucchesi, 1976), pp. 11-12. E. Campi, C. Sodini, *Gli Oriundi Lucchesi e il Cardinale Spinola* (Napoli: Prismi Editrice, 1989), p. 42.
27 M. Fulvio, *Una Famiglia Lucchese*, pp. 10-11.
28 E. de Budé, *Vita di Giovanni Diodati, Teologo Ginevrino* (Firenze: Claudiana, 1870), p. 21. P. McNair, *Pietro Martire Vermigli in Italia* (Napoli: Edizioni Centro Biblico, 1971), p. 268.
29 A. Milli, *Giovanni Diodati*, p. 43.
30 For a discussion of the actual date, see E. Campi, in *La Sacra Bibbia*, M. Ranchetti and M. Ventura eds., I, p. clxxxvii. Cf. M. Ventura, *L'Esegesi del Genesi e la Teologia della Riforma*, pp. 100-101.
31 G. Lewis, "Calvinism in Geneva in the time of Calvin and of Beza (1541-1605)," in *International Calvinism*, M. Prestwich ed. (Oxford: Clarendon Press, 1985), p. 69; emphasis added.
32 W. Stanford Reid, "Calvin and the Founding of the Academy of Geneva," *Westminster Theological Journal*, 1955, p. 8.

[33] Ibid., p. 17. "Typically humanistic" means to be trained in the classics and humanities, not what is now known as secular humanism.
[34] R. W. Wallace, *Calvin, Geneva and the Reformation* (Grand Rapids: Baker, 1988), p. 100.
[35] L. Binz, "Coup d'oeil sur l'histoire du Collège," in *Le Collège de Genève 1559-1959* (Geneve, 1959), p. 13, quoted by R. Coisson, *Giovanni Diodati e la sua Attività Ecclesiastica*, pp. 28-29.
[36] W. Stanford Reid, "Calvin and the Founding of the Academy of Geneva," p. 18.
[37] See R. M. Kingdon, *Geneva and the Coming of the Wars of Religion in France, 1555-1563* (Geneva, 1956), as quoted by A. E. McGrath, *Giovanni Calvino. Il Riformatore e la sua Influenza sulla Cultura Occidentale* (Torino: Claudiana, 1991), pp. 222-250; M. Prestwich, "Calvinism in France," in *International Calvinism*.
[38] R. M. Kingdon, *Geneva and the Coming of the Wars of Religion in France, 1555-1563*, p. 14.
[39] Ibid.
[40] Ibid.
[41] M. Ranchetti, *La Sacra Bibbia*, M. Ranchetti and M. Ventura eds., I, pp. xi-xii.
[42] E. Campi, op. cit., I, p. clxxxix.
[43] C. Borgeaud, *Histoire de l'Université de Genève*, pp. 201-202, 221-276.
[44] E. Campi, *La Sacra Bibbia*, M. Ranchetti and M. Ventura eds., I, pp. cxc-cxci.
[45] In English it would read "The Bible, Namely the Books of the Old and New Testament Newly Translated in the Italian Language by Giovanni Diodati of Lucca."
[46] W. A. McComish, *The Epigones*, p. 167. For a list of Diodati's letters, see pp. 40-41, and *La Sacra Bibbia*, M. Ranchetti and M. Ventura eds., III, pp. 1481-83. The biography by de Budé records many letters to and from Diodati.
[47] *Theses theologicae de Sacra Scriptura, quas D.O.M. auspice preside rev. et clariss. Viro D. Antonio Fayo S. S. Theologiae in celebre Genevensium Schola Professore atque ibidem ecclesiae pastore fedelissimo, publice examinandas proponit Ioannes Deodatus Genev.* (Geneva: Jean de Tournes, 1596).
[48] J. Cherbuliez, *Genève ses Institutions ses Moeurs* (Genève: 1867), p. 111, quoted by R. Coisson, *Giovanni Diodati e la sua Attività Ecclesiastica*, pp. 11-12.
[49] *The Creeds of Christendom* (Grand Rapids: Baker Book House, 1983), ed. P. Schaff, II, pp. 79-83.

50 H. Jedin, *Il Concilio di Trento: il Primo Periodo 1545-1547* (The Council of Trent: the first period 1545-1547), II (Brescia: Morcelliana, 1962), pp. 67-118.
51 G. Fragnito, *La Bibbia al Rogo* (Bologna: Il Mulino, 1997), p. 75.
52 E. de Budé, *Vie de Jean Diodati*, p. 32.
53 The majority of those who have written on Diodati affirm that there were two journeys to Venice, but the scholarly researches of Professor Emidio Campi seem to contradict this opinion. See E. Campi, *La Sacra Bibbia*, M. Ranchetti and M. Ventura eds., I, p. cxcvi.
54 The Friar Paolo Sarpi is famous for his defense of the Republic of Venice against the abuses of the Pope. Rome was so disturbed by his writings that the notorious Roberto Bellarmino was commissioned to answer him. Sarpi's writings were put on the Index and the Inquisition proclaimed him a heretic. In 1607, the Pope hired some killers to murder him, but, though he was much harmed, he survived. It seems that on more than twenty occasions the papists conspired to kill him. One of his major works is the *History of the Council of Trent,* translated into French by John Diodati himself.
55 E. de Budé, *Vie de Jean Diodati*, pp. 54-55.
56 Ibid.
57 Ibid., pp. 68-69.
58 June 24, 1608.
59 W. A. McComish, *The Epigones*, pp. 5, 189.
60 C. Dardier, "Jean Diodati a Nimes 1614," *Bulletin de la Société de l'Histoire du Protestanisme Francais,* 1853. See also E. de Budé, *Vie de Jean Diodati,* pp. 100-108; A. Milli, *Giovanni Diodati,* pp. 58-59.
61 E. Campi, *La Sacra Bibbia*, M. Ranchetti and M. Ventura eds., I, p. cc. See also E. de Budé, *Vie de Jean Diodati,* pp. 108-109.
62 R. Coisson, *Giovanni Diodati e la sua Attività Ecclesiastica*, p. 59.
63 Quoted by W. A. McComish, *The Epigones*, pp. 3, 59.
64 E. Campi, *La Sacra Bibbia*, M. Ranchetti and M. Ventura eds., I, p. ccxix.
65 Benedetto Turrettini (1588-1631), son of Francesco Turrettini – another refugee from Lucca – was the father of Francesco (Francis) Turrettini, the author of the famous *Institutio Theologiae Elencticae*. Benedetto, too, was trained at the Academy and became a distinguished professor and a pastor in Geneva. Along with Diodati and Tronchin, he is known as an "epigone." See Borgeaud, *Histoire de l'Université de Genève,* I, pp. 333-341, and W. A. McComish, *The Epigones*.
66 W. Cunningham, *The Reformers and the Theology of the Reformation* (Edinburgh: Banner of Truth, 1967), p. 366.
67 W. A. McComish, *The Epigones*, pp. 56-59.

[68] Ibid., p. 74.
[69] Coton's *Geneve plagiarie ou verification des depravations de la parole de Dieu, qui se trouvent ens Bibles de Geneve* was published in 1618. This work examined two hundred passages that, according to Coton, the Genevan pastors translated wrongly.
[70] W. A. McComish, *The Epigones*, pp. 127-145.
[71] In spite of the publication of this work, Diodati was not able to accomplish his purpose in the Italian churches scattered throughout Europe.
[72] *The Articles of the Synod of Dort*, translated from the Latin with notes by the Rev. Thomas Scott D. D., to which is added an introductory essay by the Rev. Samuel Miller D. D. (Philadelphia: 1841), p. 286.
[73] F. Turretin, *Institutes of Elenctic Theology* (Phillipsburg: Presbyterian and Reformed Publishing, 1994), II, pp. 457-458.
[74] E. Campi, *La Sacra Bibbia*, M. Ranchetti and M. Ventura eds., I, pp. ccxii-ccxiii.
[75] In 1989, an anastatic reprint of this edition was published in Italy (505 copies only) under the auspices of the British and Foreign Bible Society.
[76] For the various editions of the *Annotations*, see W. A. McComish, *The Epigones*, pp. 16-20.
[77] See Diodati's letter to the Synod of Alençon in 1637, J. Quick, *Synodicon in Gallia Reformata: or, The Acts, Decisions, Decrees and Canons of the Seven Last National Councils of the Reformed Churches in France* (London: Richardson, 1692), II, pp. 412-422.
[78] E. Campi, *La Sacra Bibbia*, M. Ranchetti and M. Ventura eds., I, p. ccvi.
[79] W. A. McComish, *The Epigones*, p. 176.
[80] Ibid., p. 177.
[81] Letter quoted in Ibid., p. 184.
[82] F. Turretin, *Institutes of Elenctic Theology*, I, p. xxxvii.
[83] The oration is given in full by C. Borgeaud, *Histoire de l'Université de Genève*, p. 462.

Chapter 2

[84] G. W. Bromiley, "The Church Fathers and Holy Scripture," in *Scripture and Truth*, eds. D. A. Carson and J. D. Woodbridge (Grand Rapids: Baker, 1992), p. 199.
[85] D. Guthrie, *New Testament Theology* (Leicester: IVP, 1981), p. 954. See also W. A. Grudem "Scripture's Self-Attestation and the Problem of Formulating a Doctrine of Scripture," in *Scripture and Truth*, eds. D. A. Carson and J. D. Woodbridge, pp. 19-59.

86 B. B. Warfield, *The Inspiration and Authority of the Bible* (Phillipsburg: Presbyterian and Reformed, 1948), p. 114.
87 Referring to *"the pattern* of sound words" mentioned in 2 Timothy 1:13 (NKJV), Joroslav Pelikan observes that the dogmatic element "was already far more explicitly at work in the first century than was once supposed" (J. Pelikan, *The Christian Tradition: A History of the Development of Doctrine,* I: *The Emergence of the Catholic Tradition, 100-600* [Chicago: University of Chicago Press, 1971], p. 70).
88 Ibid., pp. 69-70.
89 B. B. Warfield, *The Inspiration and Authority of the Bible*, p. 296.
90 J. N. D. Kelly, *Early Christian Doctrines* (New York: HarperCollins Publishers, 1978), p. 62.
91 J. Pelikan, *The Emergence of the Catholic Tradition*, pp. 72, 75.
92 B. M. Metzger, *The Canon of the New Testament, its Origin, Development and Significance* (Oxford: Clarendon Press, 1987), pp. 91-94.
93 J. Pelikan, *The Emergence of the Catholic Tradition*, p. 120.
94 Ibid., p. 79; B. M . Metzger, *The Canon of the New Testament*, p. 98.
95 J. Pelikan, *The Emergence of the Catholic Tradition*, p. 82. See also J. N. D. Kelly, *Early Christian Doctrines*, p. 26.
96 B. M. Metzger, *The Canon of the New Testament*, pp. 77-78.
97 J. Pelikan, *The Emergence of the Catholic Tradition*, p. 105.
98 B. M. Metzger, *The Canon of the New Testament*, p. 100.
99 Ibid.
100 R. A. Muller, *Post-Reformation Reformed Dogmatics*, II, *Holy Scripture: the Cognitive Foundation of Theology* (Grand Rapids: Baker Books, 1993), p. 67.
101 J. Pelikan, *The Emergence of the Catholic Tradition*, p. 243.
102 Ibid.
103 G. W. H. Lampe, "The Exposition and Exegesis of Scripture to Gregory the Great," in *The Cambridge History of the Bible*, ed. G. W. H. Lampe (Cambridge: Cambridge University Press, 1980), II, p. 163.
104 Ibid., p. 164.
105 D. S. Dockery, *Biblical Interpretation Then and Now* (Grand Rapids: Baker, 1992), p. 128; cf. G. Bray, *Biblical Interpretation Past and Present* (Downers Grove: IVP, 1996), pp. 104-111. Referring to Augustine, Lampe affirms that in his treatment of miracle stories he uses "a combination of quasi-rationalizing explanation with Origenistic allegory" (G. W. H. Lampe, *The Cambridge History of the Bible*, II, p. 180).
106 D. J. Leclercq, "The Exposition and Exegesis of Scripture From Gregory the Great to St. Bernard," in *The Cambridge History of the Bible*, II, p. 184.

[107] This refers especially to those who embraced the monastic life, far fewer of the clergy, and to very few laymen. It is well-known that the masses of Europe remained pagan in their inward religious attitudes. Gerald Bray affirms that "medieval society created a culture that was Christian . . . [but] often this meant baptizing the pagan past and recycling it in a new guise.... The Bible . . . [was] read only by scholars" (*Biblical Interpretation Past and Present*, p. 130). It was Nietzsche, speaking of Germany, who affirmed: "In medieval Germany . . . we recognize in these St. John's and St. Vitus' dancers the bacchic choruses of the Greeks, who had their precursors in Asia Minor and as far back as Babylon and the orgiastic Sacaea," *La Nascita della Tragedia* (The Birth of Tragedy from the Spirit of Music), (Milano: Adelphi Edizioni, 1972), p. 25.

[108] Ibid. See also D. J. Leclercq, *The Cambridge History of the Bible*, II, p.193.

[109] R. A. Muller, *Post-Reformation Reformed Dogmatics*, II, pp. 17-18.

[110] D. Knowles, *L'Evoluzione del Pensiero Medievale* (The Evolution of Medieval Thought), (Bologna: Il Mulino, 1984), pp.105, 125.

[111] G. Bray, *Biblical Interpretation Past and Present*, p. 148. See also R. A. Muller, *Post-Reformation Reformed Dogmatics*, II, pp. 14-15; B. Smalley, "The Bible in the Medieval Schools," *The Cambridge History of the Bible*, II, pp. 204-205.

[112] É. Gilson, *La Filosofia nel Medioevo* (Philosophy in the Middle Ages), (Firenze: La Nuova Italia, 1973), p. 303.

[113] G. Bray, *Biblical Interpretation Past and Present*, p. 149. See also R. A. Muller, *Post-Reformation Reformed Dogmatics*, II, p. 15.

[114] B. Smalley, *The Cambridge History of the Bible*, II, p. 199.

[115] G. Bray, *Biblical Interpretation Past and Present*, pp. 152-153.

[116] R. A. Muller, *Post-Reformation Reformed Dogmatics*, II, p. 20.

[117] Ibid., pp. 23-25.

[118] Quoted in Ibid., p. 33.

[119] A. E. McGrath, *Reformation Thought. An Introduction* (Oxford: Basil Blackwell, 1993), pp. 90-91 of the Italian edition (Torino: Claudiana, 1995). See also L. Bouyer, "Erasmus in Relation to the Medieval biblical tradition," in *The Cambridge History of the Bible*, II, pp. 492-493.

[120] *Calvin's Commentaries* (Grand Rapids: Baker Book House, 1996), IV, p. xl. On the date of Calvin's entrance to the university see A. McGrath, *A Life of John Calvin: A Study in the Shaping of Western Culture* (Oxford: Basil Blackwell, 1990), pp. 37-38 of the Italian edition (Torino: Claudiana, 1991).

[121] *Calvin's Commentaries*, IV, p. xl.

122 P. Schaff, *History of the Christian Church* (Grand Rapids: Eerdmans, 1988), VIII, pp. 846-848.
123 H. M. Baird, *Theodore Beza, the Counsellor of the French Reformation 1519-1605* (London: G. P. Putman's Sons, 1899), p. 10.
124 See especially B. B. Warfield, "Calvin's Doctrine of the Knowledge of God" in *Calvin and Augustine* (Phillipsburg: Presbyterian and Reformed, 1980).
125 J. Calvin, *Institutes of the Christian Religion*, I.ii.1. When not otherwise indicated, F. L. Battles' translation is used, *Calvin's Collection* (Albany: Ages Software, 1998).
126 Ibid., I.iii.1, 3; iv.1.
127 Ibid., I.v.1.
128 Ibid., I.iv.
129 Ibid., I.xi-xv.
130 Ibid., I.vi.1.
131 Ibid.
132 Ibid.
133 Ibid., I.vii.5.
134 *Calvin's Commentaries*, XVII, "The Argument to the Gospel of John," *Commentary on the Gospel According to John*, I, p. 21. The terms "dictation" and "dictated" appear in Calvin's comments on 2 Peter 1:11-12 and 2 Timothy 3:16.
135 J. Calvin, *Institutes of the Christian Religion*, trans. H. Beveridge, IV.viii.9, *Calvin's Collection*.
136 Ibid., I.vi.2.
137 *Calvin's Commentaries*, XXII, *Commentaries on the Catholic Epistles*, pp. 390-391.
138 B. B. Warfield, *Calvin and Augustine*, pp. 63-64.
139 E. A. Dowey, *The Knowledge of God in Calvin's Theology* (Grand Rapids: Eerdmans, 1994), p. 101.
140 T. Beza, "La Confession de Foi du Chrétien" in *La Revue Rèformèe*, IV, 1955.
141 P. Schaff, "History of the Creeds," in *The Creeds of Christendom* (Grand Rapids: Baker Book House, 1993), I, pp. 494-495.
142 Ibid., p. 507.
143 See D. B. Clendenin, "Orthodoxy on Scripture and Tradition: a Comparison with Reformed and Catholic Perspectives," *Westminster Theological Journal*, 57, 1995, p. 389.
144 *Confessions and Catechisms of the Reformation*, ed. M. A. Noll (Grand Rapids: Baker Book House, 1991), p. 126.
145 Muller, *Post-Reformation Reformed Dogmatics*, II, p. 40.
146 On this see H. A. Oberman, *The Dawn of the Reformation* (Edinburgh: T & Clark, 1986), p. 270.

Notes 117

[147] J. N. D. Kelly, *Early Christian Doctrines*, pp. 47-48. See also H. A. Oberman, *The Dawn of the Reformation*, pp. 270-275.

[148] Ibid., p. 277. See also J. Pelikan, *The Christian Tradition: A History of the Development of Doctrine*, IV: *Reformation of Church and Dogma, 1300-1700* (Chicago: University of Chicago Press, 1984), p. 263.

[149] Basil of Cesarea, *De Spiritu Sancto* 66, in *The Later Christian Fathers*, ed. H. Bettenson (Oxford: Oxford University Press, 1989), p. 59, emphasis added.

[150] Augustine, "Against the Epistle of Manicheus called Fundamental," *Works of Augustine*, in *Calvin's Collection*, V.6.

[151] Cf. B. B. Warfield, "Augustine's Doctrine of Knowledge and Authority," in *Calvin and Augustine*, pp. 387-477.

[152] H. A. Oberman, *The Dawn of the Reformation*, p. 281.

[153] It follows a list of the 39 books of the Old Testament with the addition of the Apocrypha and the 27 books of the New Testament.

[154] *The Creeds of Christendom*, II, pp. 79-83; emphasis added.

[155] H. A. Oberman, *The Dawn of the Reformation*, p. 288.

Chapter 4

[156] On this see the discussion of B. B. Warfield, "God-inspired Scripture," in *The Inspiration and Authority of the Bible*, pp. 285-290.

[157] *Theses Theologicae de Verbo Dei, Quas annuente foeliciter Deo, sub auspicijs Reverendi Clarissimique, viri D. Iohannis Deodati SS. Teologie in inclita Geneuensium Accademia Professoris digniùssimi, & in Ecclesia ibidem Pastoris vigilantissimi, publice defedendas susciti Iacobus Duchattus Metensis, Ad diem 17 Iuny 1620, hora locoque solitis. Geneva. Ex typographia Iohannis Plancaei, M.DC.XX.*

[158] J. Diodati, *Pious Annotations upon the Holy Bible plainly expounding the most difficult places thereof* (London: James Flesher, 3rd ed., 1651).

[159] *Annotations*, 2 Peter 1:21.

[160] R. Muller, *Post-Reformation Reformed Dogmatics*, II, pp. 231-239.

[161] *Thesis III*.

[162] *Thesis V*.

[163] R. Muller, *Post-Reformation Reformed Dogmatics*, II, pp. 249, 268.

[164] According to Reformed and post-Reformation dogmatics, the final cause of Scriptures is twofold: the glory of God and the salvation of the elect. Diodati does not make direct reference to the glory of God. Later, in 1620, his student Jaques Duchat would state clearly in his 21st thesis on *De Verbo Dei* the "double end" of Holy Scripture.

[165] *Annotations*, Romans 1:19, 21.

[166] J. Duchat, *Theses Theologicae de Verbo Dei, Thesis II*.

[167] B. M. Metzger, "Appendix I," *The Canon of the New Testament*, p. 256.
[168] R. Muller, *Post-Reformation Reformed Dogmatics*, II, p. 358.
[169] Ibid., p. 391.
[170] Augustine, "De doctrina christiana" II.12, in *The Nicene and Post-Nicene Fathers*, ed. P. Schaff, first series, II, pp. 1124-1125, in *Calvin's Collection*.
[171] R. Muller, *Post-Reformation Reformed Dogmatics*, II, pp. 394-395; emphasis added.
[172] F. J. Crehan, "The Bible in the Roman Catholic Church from Trent to the Present Day," in *The Cambridge History of the Bible*, ed. S. L. Greenslade (Cambridge: Cambridge University Press, 1963), III, p. 199.
[173] J. Calvin, *Institutes of the Christian Religion*, I.vii.1.
[174] Following this advertisement, there is an introduction to each book of the Apocrypha.
[175] R. H. Bainton, "The Bible in the Reformation," in *The Cambridge History of the Bible*, III, p. 10.
[176] Cf. R. Muller, *Post-Reformation Reformed Dogmatics*, II, pp. 418-421; 430-437, and M. Ventura, *Giovanni Diodati*, pp. 1-17.
[177] M. Ventura, *Giovanni Diodati*, p. 18.
[178] *The Creeds of Christendom*, ed. P. Schaff, II, p. 82; emphasis added.
[179] R. Muller, *Post-Reformation Reformed Dogmatics*, II, p. 420.
[180] F. J. Crehan, *The Cambridge History of the Bible*, III, p. 204.
[181] M. Ventura, *Giovanni Diodati*, pp. 134-144.
[182] J. Quick, *Synodicon in Gallia Reformata*, II, p. 421.
[183] F. Turretin, *Institutes of Elenctic Theology*, I.x.3, I, p. 106.
[184] The so-called *autographa* are defined as "the original autograph copies of the books of the Bible as they came from the hands of the inspired authors." The *apographa* are "copies of an original; specifically, the scribal copies of the original *autographa* of Scripture." See R. A. Muller, *Dictionary of Latin and Greek Theological Terms, Drawn Principally from Protestant Scholastic Theology* (Grand Rapids: Baker Book House, 1985), pp. 40, 53.
[185] F. Turretin, *Institutes of Elenctic Theology*, I.x.2, I, p. 106; emphasis added. These terms appear also, for instance, in J. Owen, *The Works of John Owen* (London: Banner of Truth, 1968), XVI, pp. 300-301.
[186] For this letter see W. A. McComish, *The Epigones*, pp. 167, 203.
[187] J. Quick, *Synodicon in Gallia Reformata*, II, p. 413.
[188] Ibid.
[189] Ibid.
[190] Manuscript in the Archivio Curia Arcivescovile di Firenze, quoted in G. Fragnito, *La Bibbia al Rogo*, p. 324; emphasis added.

191 W. A. McComish, *The Epigones*, p. 167. See also the opinion of M. Ventura, *L'Esegesi del Genesi e la Teologia della Riforma*, pp. 198-213 and *Giovanni Diodati*, pp. 44-45.
192 For a discussion on the controversy about the publication of Diodati's French Bible, see R. Coisson, *Giovanni Diodati e la sua Attività Ecclesiastica*, pp. 154-168 and W. A. McComish, *The Epigones*, pp. 175-184.
193 W. A. McComish, *The Epigones*, p. 175; emphasis added.
194 J. Quick, *Synodicon in Gallia Reformata*, II, p. 413.
195 Ibid., pp. 414-15.
196 Ibid., p. 417.
197 Ibid.
198 Ibid., p. 418.
199 Ibid., p. 419.
200 Ibid.
201 Ibid.
202 Ibid.
203 Ibid., p. 420.
204 Ibid.
205 Ibid.
206 Ibid.
207 On these events see G. Spini, *Risorgimento e Protestanti* (Risorgimento and the Protestants), (Milano: Il Saggiatore, 1989) and V. Vinay, *Storia dei Valdesi* (History of the Waldensians), III (Torino: Claudiana, 1980).
208 G. Fragnito, *La Bibbia al Rogo*, p. 9. This was the situation until the index of Benedictus XIV in 1758.
209 On the early history of the Waldensians, see A. Molnar, *Storia dei Valdesi* (Torino: Claudiana, 1989), I, esp. pp. 1-9-20, 240-42.
210 On "Vernacular Scriptures," see *The Cambridge History of the Bible*, II, pp. 338-491.
211 On the suppression of heresy in the Middle Ages before the Inquisition, see G. G. Merlo, *Contro gli Eretici* (Against Heretics), (Bologna: Il Mulino, 1996).
212 H. Hargreaves, "The Wycliffite Versions," in *The Cambridge History of the Bible*, II, pp. 393-394; emphasis added.
213 *Annotations*, Psalms 119:130.
214 F. Turretin, *Institutes of Elenctic Theology*, I.xvii.1, I, p. 143.
215 *Annotations*, Deuteronomy 30:11.
216 *Annotations*, 1 Corinthians 2:14.
217 Ibid., 1 Corinthians 2:11.
218 Ibid., 1 Corinthians 2:12.
219 Ibid., Psalm 119:18.
220 Ibid., Psalm 36:9.

[221] Ibid., 1 Corinthians 2:16.
[222] See G. Fragnito, *La Bibbia al Rogo*, p. 317.
[223] *The Creeds of Christendom*, ed. P. Schaff, II, p. 83.
[224] F. Turretin, *Institutes of Elenctic Theology*, I.xvii.1, I, p. 149.
[225] M. Ventura, *L'Esegesi del Genesi e la Teologia della Riforma*, pp. 214-17.
[226] D. S. Dockery, *Biblical Interpretation Then and Now*, p. 105.
[227] R. A. Muller, "Biblical Interpretation in the Era of the Reformation: The View from the Middle Ages," in *Biblical Interpretation in the Era of the Reformation*, pp. 8-10.
[228] Ibid., p. 12.
[229] T. H. L. Parker, *Calvin's Old Testament Commentaries* (Louisville: Westminster/John Knox, 1993), p. 70.
[230] R. A. Muller, "Biblical Interpretation in the Era of the Reformation: The View from the Middle Ages," in *Biblical Interpretation in the Era of the Reformation*, p. 9.
[231] F. Turretin, *Institutes of Elenctic Theology*, I.xvii.1, I, p. 154.
[232] *Annotations*, 1 Corinthians 2:12-16.
[233] *Annotations*, John 14:17; 15:26.
[234] *Annotations*, John 6:63.
[235] *Annotations*, John 16:13.
[236] See Calvin's comment on 2 Peter 1:20-21.
[237] *Annotations*, 2 Peter 1:20.
[238] R. Muller, *Post-Reformation Reformed Dogmatics*, II, p. 501.
[239] *Annotations*, John 6:52.
[240] M. Ventura, *L'Esegesi del Genesi e la Teologia della Riforma*, p. 221.
[241] Ibid., p. 178.
[242] Ibid., pp. 145-146.
[243] C. Borgeuad, *Histoire de l'Université de Genève*, I, pp. 200-216.
[244] F. W. Farrar, *History of Interpretation* (Grand Rapids: Baker Book House, 1961), pp. 363-365.
[245] For the results of a rejection of Diodati's view, and a modern reaffirmation of his opinions, see R. A. Muller, "The Significance of Precritical Exegesis," *Biblical Interpretation*, eds. R. A. Muller, J. L. Thompson, p. 338; D. C. Steinmetz, "The Superiority of Precritical Exegesis," in *Theology* Today, 37 (1980-81), pp. 27-38; G. Bray, *Biblical Interpretation Past and Present*, pp. 221-223, 461-588.
[246] For a listing of the external and internal marks by which Scripture proves its own divinity, see F. Turretin, *Institutes of Elenctic Theology*, I.xvii.1, I, pp. 62-64.
[247] *Annotations*, 1 Corinthians 3:10; emphasis added.
[248] See Comment on Theses XII, XIII and XIV.
[249] Cf. J. Calvin, *Institutes of the Christian Religion*, I.vii.3.
[250] *Annotations*, 1 Corinthians 2:4-5.

251 *Annotations*, 1 John 5:6.
252 F. Turretin, *Institutes of Elenctic Theology*, I.xvii.1, I, p. 87.
253 In a very challenging essay on "The Church Doctrine of Inspiration," B. B. Warfield says: "We are all of us members in particular of the body of Christ which we call the church: and the life of the church, and the faith of the church, and the thought of the church are our natural heritage. We know how, as Christian men, we approach this Holy Book, - how unquestionably we receive its statements of fact, bow before its enunciations of duty, tremble before its threatenings, and rest upon its promises . . . Our memory will easily recall those happier days when we stood a child at our Christian mother's knee, with lisping lips following the words which her slow finger traced upon this open page, - words which were her support in every trial and, as she fondly trusted, were to be our guide throughout life. *Mother church was speaking to us in that maternal voice, commending to us her vital faith in the Word of God*," in *The Inspiration and Authority if the Bible*, pp.106-107; emphasis added. In his thesis, Diodati is referring to the same 'speaking in that maternal voice" by "Mother Church" referred to by Warfield.
254 F. Turretin, *Institutes of Elenctic Theology*, I.xvii.1, I, p. 63.
255 *Annotations*, Psalm 1:2.
256 Ibid., Romans 1:16-17.
257 Ibid., John 6:27.
258 Ibid., I Peter 1:23.
259 Cf. F. Turretin, *Institutes of Elenctic Theology*, I.ii.2, I, p. 57.
260 R. Muller, *Post-Reformation Reformed Dogmatics*, II, p. 156.
261 *Annotations*, John 1:1.
262 Ibid., Hebrews 1:2.
263 Ibid., Ephesians 2:20.
264 *Annotations*, Luke 11:28; emphasis added.
265 J. Calvin, "Catechism of the Church of Geneva," *Select Works of John Calvin, Tracts and Letters*, I.ii, in *Calvin's Collection*.
266 *The Creeds of Christendom*, ed. P. Scahff, II, pp. 79-83; emphasis added.
267 F. Turretin, *Institutes of Elenctic Theology*, I.ii.16, I, p. 136.
268 *Annotations*, Matthew 15:2.
269 Ibid.
270 Ibid., Matthew 15:6.
271 Ibid., 1 Corinthians 11:2.
272 Ibid., Acts 16:4.
273 Ibid., Acts 15:20; emphasis added.
274 Ibid., Matthew 16:19; emphasis added.

[275] *Handbuch der Kichengeschichte*, ed. H. Jedin (Italian edition, Milano: Jaca Book, 1994, VI, p. 562).
[276] B. B. Warfield, "The Real Problem of Inspiration," in *The Inspiration and Authority of the Bible*, p. 226.
[277] *Annotations*, Psalm 119:66.

Conclusion

[278] S. Caponnetto, *La Riforma Protestante nell'Italia del Cinquecento*, p. 129.
[279] G. Fragnito, *La Bibbia la Rogo*, p. 16.
[280] For a list of these theses, see *La Sacra Bibbia*, M. Ranchetti and M. Ventura eds., III, pp. 1479-1481. I am indebted to Dr. Milka Ventura for having kindly sent me photocopies of all the theses discussed by Diodati's students.
[281] *Catechismo della Chiesa Cattolica* (Città del Vaticano: Libreria Editrice Vaticana, 1999), § 795, p. 239.
[282] M. Ventura, *Giovanni Diodati*, p. 44.
[283] J. Diodati, *Letter to the Academics of Saumur, 25 June 1635*, M. Ventura, *Giovanni Diodati*, Appendix, § b, p. xiii.
[284] S. Bozzola, *La Sacra Bibbia*, M. Ranchetti and M. Ventura eds., I, pp. clvii-clviii.
[285] *Diodatina* is the common name for Diodati's version of the Bible in Italian.
[286] Ibid., p. clix.
[287] Ibid., p. clxii.
[288] M. Ventura, *Giovanni Diodati*, p. 92.
[289] Ibid., p. 96.
[290] W. McComish, *The Epigones*, pp. 175-177.
[291] D. Daniell, *William Tyndale: A Biography* (New Haven: Yale University Press, 1994), pp. 1, 280.
[292] G. Spini, *Risorgimento e Protestanti*, p. 10.

BIBLIOGRAPHY

For a complete bibliography of Diodati's works, theological theses, and letters see: William A. McComish, *The Epigones: A Study of the Theology of the Genevan Academy at the Time of the Synod of Dort, with Special Reference to Giovanni Diodati* (Allison Park, PA: Pickwick Publications, 1989), pp. 227-272; *La Sacra Bibbia, Tradotta in Lingua Italiana e Commentata da Giovanni Diodati,* Michele Ranchetti e Milka Ventura eds. (Milano: Mondadori, 1999), Vol. 3, pp. 1475-1491.

Adorni Braccesi, Simonetta. *Una Città Infetta. La Repubblica di Lucca nella Crisi Religiosa del Cinquecento.* Firenze: Olschki, 1994.

Arminius, James. *The Works of James Arminius.* Grand Rapids: Baker Book House, 1991.

Articles of the Synod of Dort. Translated from the Latin with notes by the Rev. T. Scott D. D., to which is added an introductory essay by the Rev. S. Miller D. D. (Philadelphia: 1841).

Baird, Henry M. *Theodore Beza, the Counsellor of the French Reformation 1519-1605.* London: G. P. Putman's Sons, 1899.

Berengo, Marino. *Nobili e Mercanti nella Lucca del Cinquecento.* Torino: Einaudi, 1974.

Bettenson Henry, ed. *The Early Christian Fathers.* Oxford: Oxford University Press, 1987.

_____, ed. *The Later Christian Fathers.* Oxford: Oxford University Press, 1989.

Beza, Theodore. "La Confession de Foi du Chrétien," in *La Revue Reformée,* IV, 1955.

Borgeaud, Charles. *Histoire de l'Université de Genève,* I. Genève: Georg, 1900.

Bray, Gerald. *Biblical Interpretation Past and Present*. Downers Grove: IVP, 1996.

Bromiley, Geoffrey W. "The Church Fathers and Holy Scripture," in *Scripture and Truth*, eds. D. A. Carson and J. D. Woodbridge. Grand Rapids: Baker, 1992.

_____. *Historical Theology: An Introduction*. Edinburgh: T&T Clark, 1994.

Brown, Harold O. J. *Heresies: the Image of Christ in the Mirror of Heresy and Orthodoxy from the Apostles to the Present*. Grand Rapids: Baker Book House, 1984.

de Budé, Emile. *Vie de Jean Diodati, Theologien Genevois*. Lousanne: Georges Bridel Editeur, 1869.

Calvin, John. *Calvin's Commentaries*. Grand Rapids: Baker Book House, 1996.

_____. *Institutes of the Christian Religion*. Albany: Ages Software, 1998.

Cambridge History of the Bible, eds. P. R. Ackroyd and C. F. Evans. Vol. 1. Cambridge: Cambridge University Press, 1970.

Cambridge History of the Bible, ed. G. W. H. Lampe. Vol. 2. Cambridge: Cambridge University Press, 1969.

Cambridge History of the Bible, ed. S. L. Greenslade. Vol. 3. Cambridge: Cambridge University Press, 1963.

Campi, Emidio and Sodini, Carla. *Gli Oriundi Lucchesi e il Cardinale Spinola*. Napoli: Prismi Editrice, 1989.

Cantimori, Delio et al. *Ginevra e l'Italia*. Firenze: Sansoni, 1959.

Caponetto, Salvatore. *La Riforma Protestante nell'Italia del Cinquecento*. Torino: Claudiana, 1992.

Catechismo della Chiesa Cattolica. Città del Vaticano: Libreria Editrice Vaticana, 1999.

Church, Frederic C., *The Italian Reformers, 1534-1564*. New York: Columbia University Press, 1932.

Bibliography 125

Clendenin, Daniel. B. "Orthodoxy on Scripture and Tradition: A Comparison with Reformed and Catholic Perspectives," *Westminster Theological Journal*, 57 (1995).

Coisson, Renato. "Giovanni Diodati e la sua Attività Ecclesiastica." Unpublished thesis, Rome: Facoltà Valdese di teologia, 1964.

Cunningham, William. *The Reformers and the Theology of the Reformation*. Edinburgh: Banner of Truth, 1967.

_____. *Historical Theology*. Edinburgh: Banner of Truth, 1960.

Daniell, David. *William Tyndale: A Biography*. New Haven: Yale University Press, 1994.

Dockery, David S. *Biblical Interpretation Then and Now*. Grand Rapids: Baker, 1992.

Dowey, Edward A. *The Knowledge of God in Calvin's Theology*. Grand Rapids: Eerdmans, 1994.

Farrar, Frederic W. *History of Interpretation*. Grand Rapids: Baker Book House, 1961.

Fragnito, Gigliola. *La Bibbia al Rogo*. Bologna: Il Mulino, 1997.

Fulvio, Manlio. *Una Famiglia Lucchese: i Diodati*. Lucca: Actum Luce, Rivista di Studi Lucchesi, 1983.

di Gangi, Mariano. *Peter Martyr Vermigli 1499-1562: Renaissance Man, Reformation Master*. Lanham: University Press of America, 1993.

Gilson, Étienne. *La Filosofia nel Medioevo*. Firenze: La Nuova Italia, 1973.

Grudem, Wayne A. "Scripture's Self-Attestation and the Problem of Formulating a Doctrine of Scripture," in *Scripture and Truth*, eds. D. A. Carson and J. D. Woodbridge. Grand Rapids: Baker, 1992.

Guthrie, Donald. *New Testament Theology*. Leicester: IVP, 1981.

Heyer, Henri. *L'Eglise de Geneve: Esquisse Historique de son Organisation*. Nieuwkoop: B. De Graaf, 1974.

Heppe, Heinrich. *Reformed Dogmatics*. London: Wakeman Trust (no date).

Hodge, Charles. *Systematic Theology*. Grand Rapids: Eerdmans, 1989.

Hugon, Armando A. *Storia dei Valdesi*, II. Torino: Claudiana, 1989.

Jedin, Hubert. *Il Concilio di Trento: il Primo Periodo 1545-1547*, II. Brescia: Morcelliana, 1962.

_____, ed. *Storia della Chiesa: Riforma e Controriforma*, VI. Milano: Jaca Book, 1994.

Kelly, John N. D. *Early Christian Doctrines*. New York: HarperCollins Publishers, 1978.

Knowles, David. *L'Evoluzione del Pensiero Medievale*. Bologna: Il Mulino, 1984.

Lewis, Gilian. "Calvinism in Geneva in the Time of Calvin and of Beza (1541-1605)," in *International Calvinism*, ed. M. Prestwich. Oxford: Clarendon Press, 1985.

Luzzati, Michele. *La Prima Generazione dei Burlamacchi a Ginevra*. Lucca: Actum Luce, Rivista di Studi Lucchesi, 1976.

Luzzi, Giovanni. *La Bibbia in Italia. L'Eco della Riforma nella Repubblica Lucchese: Giovanni Diodati e la sua Traduzione Italiana della Bibbia*. Firenze: Claudiana, 1942.

_____. *The Struggle for Christian Truth in Italy*. New York: Fleming H. Revell, 1913.

McComish, William A. *The Epigones: A Study of the Theology of the Genevan Academy at the Time of the Synod of Dort, with Special Reference to Giovanni Diodati*. Allison Park: Pickwick Publications, 1989.

McGrath, Alister E. *Giovanni Calvino. Il Riformatore e la sua Influenza sulla Cultura Occidentale*. Torino: Claudiana, 1991.

_____. *Il Pensiero della Riforma*. Torino: Claudiana, 1995.

McNair, Philip. *Pietro Martire Vermigli in Italia*. Napoli: Edizioni Centro Biblico, 1971.

Merlo, Grado G. *Contro gli Eretici*. Bologna: Il Mulino, 1996.

_____. *Eretici ed Eresie medievali*. Bologna: Il Mulino, 1989.

Metzger, Bruce M. *The Canon of the New Testament, its Origin, Development and Significance.* Oxford: Clarendon Press, 1987.

Milli, Angiolo. *Giovanni Diodati il Traduttore della Bibbia e la Società degli Esuli Protestanti Italiani a Ginevra 1560-1660.* Lausanne: G. Amacker, 1908.

Molnar, Amedeo. *Storia dei Valdesi,* I. Torino: Claudiana, 1989.

Muller, Richard A. *Christ and the Decree.* Durham, N.C.: Labyrinth Press, 1986.

_____. *Dictionary of Latin and Greek Theological Terms, Drawn Principally from Protestant Scholastic Theology.* Grand Rapids: Baker Book House, 1985.

_____. *Post-Reformation Reformed Dogmatics.* 4 vols. Grand Rapids: Baker Books, 1993-2003.

_____, and J. E. Bradley, eds. *Church History: An Introduction to Research, Reference Works, and Methods.* Grand Rapids: Eerdmans, 1995.

_____, and J. L. Thompson, eds. *Biblical Interpretation in the Era of Reformation.* Grand Rapids: Eerdmans, 1996.

Noll, Mark A. ed. *Confessions and Catechisms of the Reformation.* Grand Rapids: Baker Book House, 1991.

Oberman, Heiko A. *The Dawn of the Reformation.* Edinburgh: T & T Clark, 1986.

_____. *The Impact of the Reformation.* Edinburgh: T&T Clark, 1994.

_____. *Masters of the Reformation.* Cambridge: Cambridge University Press, 1981.

_____. *The Reformation: Roots and Ramification.* Edinburgh: T&T Clark, 1994.

Orr, James. *The Progress of Dogma.* Vancouver: Regent College Publishing, 2000.

Owen, John. *The Works of John Owen,* vol. 16. London: Banner of Truth, 1968.

Parker, Thomas H. L. *Calvin's Old Testament Commentaries.* Louisville: Westminster/John Knox, 1993.

_____. *Calvin's New Testament Commentaries*. Louisville: Westminster/John Knox, 1993.

Pascal, Arturo. *Da Lucca a Ginevra: Studi sull'Emigrazione Religiosa Lucchese nel sec. XVI*. Torino: Paravia, 1932.

Pelikan, Jeroslav. *The Christian Tradition: The Emergence of the Catholic tradition, 100-600*. Chicago: University of Chicago Press, 1971.

_____. *The Christian Tradition: The Spirit of Eastern Christendom, 600-1700*. Chicago: University of Chicago Press, 1974.

_____. *The Christian Tradition: The Growth of Medieval Theology, 600-1300*. Chicago: University of Chicago Press, 1978.

_____. *The Christian Tradition: Reformation of Church and Dogma, 1300-1700*. Chicago: University of Chicago Press, 1984.

Peyronel, Susanna, ed. *Cinquant'anni di Storiografia Italiana sulla Riforma e i Movimenti Ereticali in Italia, 1950-2000*. Torino: Claudiana, 2002.

Prestwich, Menna. "Calvinism in France," in *International Calvinism*. Oxford: Clarendon Press, 1985.

Quick, John. *Synodicon in Gallia Reformata: or, The Acts, Decisions, Decrees and Canons of the Seven Last National Councils of the Reformed Churches in France*. London: Richardson, 1692.

Schaff, Philip. *History of the Christian Church*. Grand Rapids: Eerdmans, 1988.

_____, ed. *The Creeds of Christendom*. Grand Rapids: Baker Book House, 1983.

Spini, Giorgio. *Risorgimento e Protestanti*. Milano: Il Saggiatore, 1989.

_____. *Storia dell'Età Moderna*. Torino: Einaudi, 1982.

Stanford Reid, William. "Calvin and the Founding of the Academy of Geneva," *Westminster Theological Journal*, 1955.

Steinmetz, David C. *Calvin in Context*. Oxford: Oxford University Press, 1995.

_____. "The Superiority of Pre-critical Exegesis," *Theology Today*, 37 (1980-81).

Turretin, Francis. *Institutes of Elenctic Theology*. 3 vols. Phillipsburg: Presbyterian and Reformed Publishing, 1994.

_____. *Notice Biographique sur Bénédict Turretini: Théologien genevois du XVII siècle*. Genève: Soullier & Wirth, 1871.

Ventura, Milka. "L'Esegesi del Genesi e la Teologia della Riforma. Due Commentari a Confronto: Brucioli e Diodati." Unpublished graduate thesis: University of Florence, 1985.

_____. "Giovanni Diodati e le Traduzioni della Bibbia nel suo Tempo: l'Antico Testamento." Unpublished doctoral thesis: University of Turin, 1993.

_____, and M. Ranchetti, eds. *La Sacra Bibbia, Tradotta in Lingua Italiana e Commentata da Giovanni Diodati*. Milano: Mondadori, 1999.

Vinay, Valdo. *Storia dei Valdesi*, III. Torino: Claudiana, 1980.

Wallace, Ronald W. *Calvin, Geneva and the Reformation*. Grand Rapids: Baker, 1988.

Warfield, Benjamin B. *Calvin and Augustine*. Phillipsburg: Presbyterian and Reformed, 1980.

_____. *The Inspiration and Authority of the Bible*. Phillipsburg: Presbyterian and Reformed, 1948.

www.ingramcontent.com/pod-product-compliance
Lightning Source LLC
Chambersburg PA
CBHW021112080526
44587CB00010B/493